OUR
CENTURY
IN
PICTURES

OUR
CENTURY
IN
PICTURES

EDITED BY RICHARD B. STOLLEY

TONY CHIU, DEPUTY EDITOR AND WRITER

A BULFINCH PRESS BOOK

LITTLE, BROWN AND COMPANY · BOSTON NEW YORK

21

68

86

116

151

Contents

209

242

317

373

416

Dust Bowls and Other Dreams

BY RICHARD B. STOLLEY, EDITOR

DON'T LOOK BACK, Satchel Paige advised, something may be gaining on you. Those of us who produced this book had no choice. While everyone else seemed to be breaking out party hats for the next millennium, we were steeping ourselves in the final century of the one fast slipping by.

Other fine books about the century use images to supplement the text. We went at the job the other way around. We were determined to tell the story in photographs. Our book has important words, of course — nine provocative essays by distinguished authors, information-rich captions for each of the 770 or so photographs. But we wanted pictures to carry the narrative; we felt that Americans today are visually sophisticated enough to read photographs and fully comprehend the information and emotion they impart. As our title promises, this is truly a picture history of the last 100 years.

We have divided the century into nine epochs, our book into nine chapters. We tell the story as the world lived it, chronologically. Within each epoch is a special section called Turning Point. Here, we put a key event in context by looking back in time at its antecedents, as well as forward in time to assess its impact. And following each epoch is Requiem, a roll call of some important newsmakers, especially cultural ones, who died during those years.

Deciding which pictures to use was a monumental, and agonizing, task. They came from the massive Time Inc. picture collection and from other archives around the world. We figure we inspected some 50,000 photographs; fewer than two percent of them made it into our book.

This immersion in the past had a peculiar effect on me. I found myself living those years during the day and dreaming about them at night. My dreams ranged across the century: One night I was a frightened doughboy in France; another, a Dust Bowl farmer hopefully heading west; a third, a laid-back dweller in a Sixties commune.

For all of us, the history lessons contained in the pictures were perhaps not surprising but overwhelmingly clear. Ours was an appallingly violent century; the death and destruction were almost beyond human comprehension. Yet again and again we discovered what Wordsworth described as the "little, nameless, unremembered acts of kindness and of love." And in the midst of worldwide terror, we saw evidence of astonishing ingenuity in science and the arts all around the beleaguered globe.

In selecting the pictures, we wanted to use the famous and familiar, yet illuminate them with companion images. Thus, you'll see the flag raising on Iwo Jima and a haunting picture of doomed Marines taken a few minutes later; the brave Chinese youth stopping the tanks in Tiananmen Square and then,

Reporting on the U.S. nuclear submarine base at Holy Loch, Scotland, in late March 1969, Dick Stolley, 41, was photographed on the deck of a sub about to embark on a 90-day Cold War patrol mission. He recalls, "Everyone topside was required to wear a life jacket because the wind — which the sailors called 'the hawk' — was strong enough to blow you overboard."

BILL RAY / LIFE

jured pilot Orville Wright; the room where the Czar and his family were murdered, its walls pocked with bullet holes; Walt Disney and his staff unself-consciously wearing, of all Hollywood outfits, knickers, every last man; invading Soviet tanks lined up on a Prague side street like taxicabs, while shoppers casually stroll by.

Personally, this book is a kind of retrospective on my life as a journalist. I covered many of the events portrayed herein — among them, the Southern civil rights struggle, Elvis in his early days, Israeli-Arab combat along the Suez Canal, JFK's death in Dallas, the search for early man in Kenya. (I still have a handful of two-million-year-old crocodile bones from that assignment.) I was actually present when some of the pictures were taken — integration in Little Rock, the H-bomb test high above the Pacific, street rioting in Paris, arming nuclear subs in Scotland.

For you, as it has been for me, I hope this book will be a keepsake, a provoker of memories, a guide to how things and people behaved and looked in the 20th Century.

Permit me one final observation. It is the remarkable extent to which the United States for the past 100 years has been spared so much of the misery inflicted elsewhere in the world. Our soldiers died, but rarely our civilians. Our cities were never bombed. Since 1865, we have endured internal strife but have not taken up arms against ourselves. We still suffer from the sordid legacy of slavery, but at home we are mostly at peace. God has indeed shed his grace on us, from sea to shining sea.

incredibly, climbing up on one to plead with the crew; the weeping Navy accordionist playing for the fallen Franklin D. Roosevelt, while a heartbreaking phalanx of the president's fellow polio victims line up in their wheelchairs to say farewell too; a rarely seen sequence of events just before and after a South Vietnamese general shockingly executed a Vietcong suspect on a Saigon street.

Finding pictures that were surprising and fresh was a constant wonder. Just to pick a disparate few: the first fatal airplane crash, which also badly in-

Joining Life *magazine in 1953, Richard B. Stolley served as chief of its bureaus in Atlanta, Los Angeles, Washington and Paris, and later as its editor. He was founding editor of* People *magazine in 1974 and then editorial director of the parent company, Time Inc., for which he is now senior editorial adviser.*

Slipping the surly bonds of earth, Wilbur Wright, 35,
piloted a glider above North Carolina in 1902. Next
challenge for him and kid brother Orville: powered flight.

1900–1913

ACROSS THE THRESHOLD

Rough-Riding into American Hearts

BY H.W. BRANDS

THE NATION NEEDED HEROES. Thirty-five years after Appomattox, the supply of Civil War heroes was slipping badly. The frontier was vanishing and with it the prospect of additional Daniel Boones and David Crocketts. The swelling cities swallowed individuals, erasing their faces and their freedom of action. Industrialization made men mere parts, interchangeable cogs in schemes far beyond their control.

What passed for heroes in that anonymizing age were the captains of industry: Carnegie, Rockefeller, Morgan. Carnegie's courage had been measured in the Battle of Homestead, waged by his hired army against his own Pennsylvania steelworkers while little Andy took his holiday in Scotland. Rockefeller's signal accomplishment consisted in cornering kerosene and making vassals of the millions who had the effrontery to wish to light their homes at night. Morgan commanded the money that commanded everything else; in the latest financial panic he had held hostage the very Treasury of the United States till President Cleveland met his exacting conditions. How high the ransom ran, Morgan disdained to reveal.

The people ached for a champion, one who could best the moguls and restore the promise of American democracy. Some thought they saw him in William Jennings Bryan, the silver-throated, iron-lunged orator from the plains of Nebraska. But the moguls and

their political allies scorched the earth around Bryan's 1896 candidacy for president, and power remained safely with the interests.

And then, like a bolt from the clear Cuban sky in the summer of 1898, a national hero, a popular champion, appeared. Theodore Roosevelt led his Rough Riders up the San Juan Heights and onto the plateau of American popularity — indeed, American adulation. The politicos tried to co-opt him by making him the Republican nominee for New York governor; but upon winning that office, he instantly exhibited the independent spirit expected of the Dakota ranchman he had been before the Spanish-American War. Thereupon the bosses sought to imprison him in the vice presidency, only to rue their choice when William McKinley died and "that damned cowboy" — in boss Mark Hanna's derisive phrase — assumed the highest office in the land.

During the first dozen years of the 20th Century, Theodore Roosevelt dominated American national life as no one had dominated it before. He was an arresting presence — that muscular figure, forever in motion; the blue eyes blazing behind his spectacles, transfixing friends with their exuberance and foes with their intensity; the teeth that bit his words like tenpenny nails and snapped defiance at all who trespassed upon the public interest.

Roosevelt was a character who became a caricature without ceasing to be a force. Acquaintances, in-

Moving into the White House with Teddy Roosevelt was the largest First Family ever. In this 1903 portrait, the President, then 44, posed with, from left: Quentin, 5; Theodore Jr., 16; Archibald, 9; Alice, 19; Kermit, 13; his second wife, Edith, 42; and Ethel, 12.

deed, likened him to a force of nature; Henry Adams called him "pure act." Roosevelt announced his presence in the White House by declaring war on J. Pierpont Morgan's newest brainchild, the Northern Securities railroad trust. Morgan had opened the new century by unveiling the world's first billion-dollar corporation, U.S. Steel; Wall Street thought him invulnerable to presidents and other mere mortals. But David slung his stones, the people cheered, and —

when the Supreme Court sided with TR and the people against Morgan and money — Goliath fell.

Roosevelt employed equal energy against big capital in a 1902 anthracite strike, threatening to use federal troops to keep the coal supply from failing and the nation from freezing. He reined in railroad rates and safeguarded the nation's food supply. He recaptured America's forests for America's people and harnessed the waterways of the West to the needs of Western farmers. He launched a successful assault on the biggest monopoly of all, Rockefeller's Standard Oil. In America's name he seized the Panama Canal Zone and started digging. He ap-

The fortune amassed by J.P. Morgan, here with daughter Louisa and son J.P. Jr., would today trail only those of Bill Gates and Warren Buffet. Among his holdings: England's White Star Line. In 1912, Morgan, 75, booked onto *Titanic*'s maiden voyage but canceled at the last minute.
TIME INC.

pointed America the policeman of the Western Hemisphere. He established himself as arbiter between Russia and Japan in northeastern Asia — and won a Nobel Peace Prize for his pains.

Americans loved Roosevelt. They elected him by a historic margin in 1904 and would have re-elected him in 1908 had he not, with uncharacteristic modesty, forsworn another race. They hung on his hunting exploits in Africa after he left the presidency ("Let every lion do his duty" was the toast among the Morgan crowd as TR's boat left New York), and upon his return they demanded another try for the top. When the Republican bosses once more stood against him, he broke ranks and fashioned his own party, aptly nicknamed Bull Moose. At the climax of the 1912 campaign an aspiring assassin shot him; bloodied but undaunted, he staggered to the finish in the strongest third-party showing in American history.

Roosevelt's hold on the American psyche said

much about him; it said more about the America of his era. America was not what it had been, and daily it was becoming less so. Cities replaced country at the nation's center of moral gravity; factories out-muscled farms. Immigrants by the millions swarmed the ports, planting cultural and linguistic beach-heads of their homelands on American shores. Radical labor unionists agitated for social revolution. Race riots and lynchings ravaged not simply the South but the Midwestern heartland of the country, sparing not even Springfield, Illinois, the home of the Great Emancipator, Abraham Lincoln. Muck-raking journalists revealed the insidious influence of money in politics, the corruption that mocked America's attachment to democracy.

Even the good news was unsettling. Henry Ford's Model T put the nation on wheels but in doing so changed the face of cities and small towns across the land — besides creating a rolling threat to life and limb. Frederick Taylor's gospel of "scientific management" boosted industrial output but dead-ened the souls of workers so scientifically managed. A revolution in printing technology drove down the price of newspapers, but competition for advertising to pay off the new presses drove down the editorial quality of the papers. Rural free delivery brought newspapers and magazines to farms but helped ho-mogenize American culture. Burgeoning industries opened new job opportunities for women but also sucked in thousands of children — and produced such workplace disasters as the appalling Triangle Shirtwaist fire of 1911.

The new century was carrying America forward, but with each step forward the country seemed to take a half step back. Reformers hopefully hitching themselves to the label "progress" sought to secure the benefits of industrialization while mitigating its costs. The progressives applied scientific manage-ment concepts to government, creating commissions and councils of the middle class to break the hold of immigrant-backed bosses. Progressive editors like S.S. McClure employed the new printing technology to price their magazines at a dime and propagate their message to millions formerly beyond the reach of quality journals. Progressive lawyers like Louis Brandeis brought sociology and economics to the courtroom to defend statutes designed to end monopolistic practices and unsafe working conditions.

Yet though the progressives had a program, as a group they lacked the ability to inspire passion. Belligerent nickname and aggressive coiffure notwithstanding, "Battling Bob" La Follette hardly set hearts pounding with his "Wisconsin idea" of political and economic reform. Nor could ordinary Americans get exercised over initiative, referendum and recall.

What progressivism needed was a compelling persona — which was precisely what it got in Theodore Roosevelt. Roosevelt was the real thing — cowboy, war hero, fierce foe of vested interests — but he was also a master at magnifying his popular appeal. Intuitively appreciating the possibilities of modern journalism, he cultivated the press, winning over reporters by the force of his personality and making them almost co-conspirators in his efforts on behalf of the American people. He showed off his family, the most boisterous bunch ever to occupy the White House. He christened the "bully pulpit" and preached from it regularly. His hunting trips (including the famous Mississippi bear hunt at which he spared what became the prototype for the teddy bear), his reunions with his Rough Rider comrades, his obvious delight ("Dee-lighted!" sprang from his mouth even more often than "Bully!") in mingling with farmers, loggers, miners, factory workers — all of this honestly reflected the person he was, but it also amplified the persona he adopted.

Roosevelt's appeal rested on his ability to bridge two eras. His heroic persona was a throwback to the 19th Century, which grew the more heroic the far-

America in 1900 consisted of the Lower 45. Still territories: Oklahoma, Arizona and New Mexico. Alaska, bought from Russia in 1867 for $7.2 million, was aswarm with gold rushers. And Hawaii, handed over by pineapple king Sanford Dole after he wrested the islands from Queen Liliuokalani, had been a U.S. possession for only two years.
CULVER PICTURES

ther it receded into romantic memory. Yet his progressive politics were solidly anchored in the 20th Century, and his ability to put across his persona relied on techniques unavailable to his predecessors.

The nation needed heroes — precisely because heroes, as it had known them, were unsuited to what the nation was becoming. Pierpont Morgan, the marshal of finance, was more characteristic of the new century than Teddy Roosevelt, the colonel of the First Volunteer Cavalry. At some level Americans understood this; after all, they had made Morgan and Carnegie and Rockefeller rich. But Americans didn't like what this said about them as a people. Roosevelt represented traditional values and tested truths, items always in demand in America, and never more in demand than during the unnerving first decade of what promised to be a most unsettling century.

H.W. Brands is the author of 14 books, including T.R.: The Last Romantic *(1997) and* Masters of Enterprise *(1999). He is Thomas Professor in Liberal Arts at Texas A&M University.*

MAJESTIC TWILIGHT

As the 20th Century dawned, the four rulers pictured here governed three out of every five human beings alive. Their world was less populous (1.6 billion versus almost six billion now) and divided into fewer sovereign states (some 50 versus today's 190 plus). But their kingdoms, so dominant for centuries, were about to be engulfed by a global quest for independence. Revolutions swept out the Chinese and the Russian dynasties. The Ottoman Empire crumbled after World War I. And in 1997, when Hong Kong reverted to China, the sun finally set on the British Empire.

<
ABDUL HAMID II

The Ottoman sultanate he inherited in 1876, at age 34, was just a husk of the mighty Islamic empire that in the 16th Century, under Sulayman the Magnificent, reached from eastern Europe to Persia and down to Arabia. Abdul Hamid II ruled erratically from the seclusion of his Istanbul palace until deposed in 1909 by the reformist Young Turks. He died in 1918, at about the same time as the 600-year-old Ottoman Empire, which was dissolved by various World War I peace treaties.

ARCHIVE PHOTOS

<
VICTORIA

In 1837, one month after her 18th birthday, she became Queen of the United Kingdom of Great Britain and Ireland. Hers was a prosperous realm thanks to the ongoing Industrial Revolution, which England had launched. Hers was also the greatest colonial empire of the 19th Century, which she expanded even farther, taking in 1876 the title of Empress of India. By her achievements and her length of reign — 63 years, the longest in English history — Victoria rightly lent her name to an age.

TIME INC.

NICHOLAS II

On becoming, at 26, the 18th in the Romanov line to rule Russia since 1613, Nicholas immediately took as his czarina Alexandra (right), a granddaughter of Queen Victoria. He proved a better husband than monarch. Comfortable only with his family and inner court, Nicholas was easily swayed by advisers like the semiliterate faith healer Rasputin. Isolated from his subjects, he had no grasp of the vast unrest that would lead to the Russian Revolution of 1917 — and to the violent end of the Romanov succession (see page 58).

TIME INC.

<
TZ'U-HSI

No other concubine ever amassed the influence of China's notorious Empress Dowager. Tz'u-hsi began ruling the country in 1862, when her six-year-old son by Emperor Hsieng-feng ascended to the throne. Then 27, she remained in power even after his death and the failure of the Boxer Rebellion, the 1900 anti-Western uprising she encouraged. Nor did Tz'u-hsi ever stop scheming. In 1908, from her sickbed, she ordered that the then emperor — her nephew — be poisoned. He died a day before she did.

TIME INC.

IN THE LINE OF DUTY

Having overseen the U.S.'s 1898 vanquishing of Spain (the victor's spoils: Cuba, Puerto Rico, Guam, the Philippines), William McKinley (near right) easily won a second term. He served only six months of it. On September 6, 1901, while visiting Buffalo, the 25th president became the third to be shot (after Lincoln and Garfield). McKinley, 58, lived eight more days; his assassin, 28-year-old anarchist Leon Czolgosz (far right), another 53 until he was sent to the electric chair.

RIGHT AND FAR RIGHT: TIME INC.

BIRTH OF A CLASSIC

On New Year's Day, 1902, 8,500 college football fans — some on horseback — watched the inaugural Rose Bowl in Pasadena, California. Every play on offense was a run; forward passes were illegal until 1906. And touchdowns and field goals both counted five points. Under any rules, it was a blowout: University of Michigan 49, Stanford 0.

BENTLEY HISTORICAL LIBRARY

<

ULTIMATE SACRIFICE

Four warriors of China's Righteous Harmony Fist movement were put to the sword in 1900 by the Japanese officer wiping clean his blade. The so-called Boxers were encouraged by the Empress Dowager to purge the Middle Kingdom of meddlesome foreigners and Christians. Their fatal mistake: attacking Western legations in Beijing. Eight nations quickly sent firearm-toting troops to crush the sword-wielding rebels.

AMERICAN MUSEUM OF
NATURAL HISTORY

TOUCHES OF CLASS

Though blind, deaf and mute before age 2, Helen Keller (near right) was, by 22, enough of a celebrity to pose with renowned actor Joseph Jefferson (far right) in 1902. She was then attending Radcliffe College, from which she graduated cum laude. Keller's real teacher was Anne Sullivan (center), the partially blind "miracle worker" only 14 years older than the pupil she had drawn into the world. Sullivan also interpreted for Keller at college and later accompanied her on world tours to promote rights for the disabled.

TIME INC.

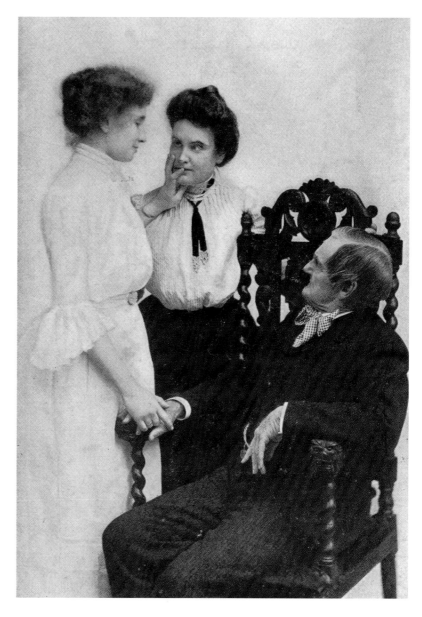

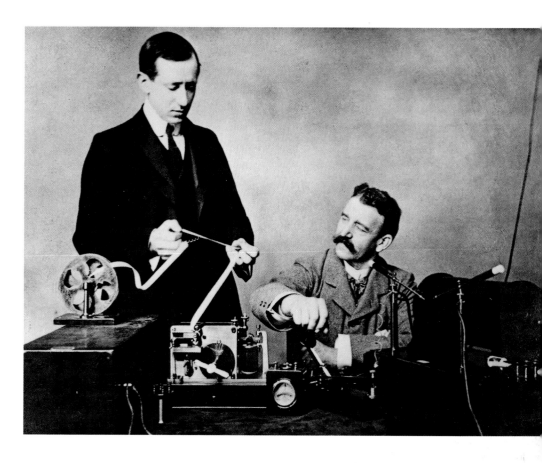

TALE OF THE TAPE

Dot-dot-dot (Morse for the letter *S*) was what the 27-year-old Guglielmo Marconi (near right) and aide G.S. Kemp received on December 12, 1901. The moment was thought historic enough to restage for this photo because the two had been in Newfoundland — and the code sent from Cornwall, England, 1,800 miles away. The Italian-Irish Marconi won the 1909 physics Nobel for his contributions to the infant medium of radio.

PIX INC.

<

ALL WASHED UP

Fifty years after Millard Fillmore stunned the nation by having a tub put in the White House, many U.S. cities boasted public facilities (few as grand as San Francisco's Sutro Baths). The aim: to improve the hygiene of the working class (fees were typically a dime). At the turn of the century, however, even the homes of the rich usually lacked running water.

NATIONAL ARCHIVES

SAY CHEESE . . .

What does *Kodak* stand for? Nothing; the trade name was fabricated by George Eastman in 1888 because he liked the letter *K*. The ex–bank clerk, then 26, went on to invent ever-better film and cameras. No Kodak product had more impact than his 1900 box Brownie, which fulfilled Eastman's wish to make "the camera as convenient as the pencil."

EASTMAN KODAK CO.

THE WRIGHT STUFF

Yes, the brothers Wright were inventors — but they were also businessmen. After all, it was in their bicycle shop in Dayton, Ohio, that Wilbur and Orville fabricated their flying machines. They did have the foresight to position a photographer to document *Wright Flyer*'s first journey. But after extensively testing *Flyer No. 2* in the summer of 1904, they shunned the limelight to work out improvements — and to patent their designs. Not until 1908 did they go public by way of field trials for the U.S. Army (a $25,000 contract) and for the French (who paid them $100,000).

WE HAVE LIFTOFF
After rolling down a 60-foot track, Orville Wright, 32, soared past Wilbur and into history. That first powered flight, on December 17, 1903, at Kill Devil Hills, North Carolina, ended after 12 seconds and spanned all of 120 feet. But the last of the day's four trials covered an impressive 852 feet.

TIME INC.

KNIGHTS OF LAND AND AIR

On a 1909 tour of Europe to promote their invention, the Wrights met automaker — and flying enthusiast — Charles Rolls (at the wheel of a six-cylinder Rolls-Royce; others pictured are, from left, Orville, patent agent Griffith Brewer and Wilbur). The next year Rolls became the first to fly across the English Channel and back nonstop. A month later he crashed and became, at 32, Britain's first air fatality.

TIME INC.

FATAL LANDING

Observers at the 1908 Army trials of the Wrights' two-man plane in Virginia hoisted the wreckage of the downed craft to free pilot Orville, who emerged with a broken leg, hip and ribs. The men at far right were tending to his passenger, who was not so fortunate; Lieutenant Thomas Selfridge died of head injuries, the first victim of the air age. Cause of the crash: One of the new extra-long wooden propellers split. Though the Wrights had made flights as long as 70 minutes, the Army was more interested in speed. To pass these trials, the plane had to average a dangerous 40 mph.

SMITHSONIAN INSTITUTION

STRANGE OLYMPICS

As part of the world's fair in St. Louis, the 1904 Olympic Games included such embarrassing events as this pole climb (and mud fighting too) designed to showcase the talents of "indigenous" people, including American Indians and African pygmies. Only 12 countries and fewer than 700 athletes bothered to compete. The Olympics remained a sideshow until the Paris Games of 1924.

IOC ARCHIVES

MEET ME IN ST. LOUIS

Anchoring the 1904 Louisiana Purchase Exposition were 10 ornate palaces scattered across a 1,200-acre site in downtown St. Louis. Never mind that this world's fair, to mark the centennial of a real-estate deal even sweeter than that for Manhattan, opened a year late. Sixty-two nations and 43 states mounted exhibits, among them the actual log cabin in which Abraham Lincoln was born. The Expo's best innovation: the ice-cream cone.

TIME INC.

ART TAKES A NEW SHAPE

Western painters were searching for new directions when a 26-year-old Spaniard set on canvas a radical, form-fracturing vision. From 1907's *Les Demoiselles d' Avignon* sprang Cubism — though for years Pablo Picasso, unsure of what he had wrought, showed the work only to close friends. Nor was it put on public exhibition until 1916.

MUSEUM OF MODERN ART

<

A CITY TUMBLES DOWN

Thirty-five years after Mrs. O'Leary's cow was blamed for the Chicago Fire, the Quake of 1906 totaled San Francisco. The main tremor on April 18 lasted less than a minute but was thought to have neared 8.3 on the Richter scale (invented in 1935, with a top value of 10). Worse was the blaze that began shortly after this photo was taken. When the last flames were put out three days later, as many as 3,000 were dead or missing, and 225,000 — more than half the city's residents — were homeless.

NOAA / EDS

FOOL FOR LOVE

At 16, Pittsburgh-born chorus-liner Evelyn Nesbit took as her sugar daddy New York architect Stanford White (whose works include the Washington Square Arch). At 19, she married mining scion Harry Thaw. He couldn't handle Nesbit's tales of rough sex with White and so in 1906 shot her former lover dead. America's first Trial of the Century ended with Thaw adjudged insane.

RUDOLF EICKEMEYER / SMITHSONIAN INSTITUTION

THE GERM SPREADER

Irish-born Mary Mallon easily found work in New York as a cook. Alas, the wealthy families she fed often took ill. In 1907, public health officials found Mallon, then 38, to be infected with typhoid while remaining herself unaffected. Dubbed Typhoid Mary by the press, she used aliases to keep cooking until 1915, when the state institutionalized her for life.

CORBIS /BETTMANN-UPI

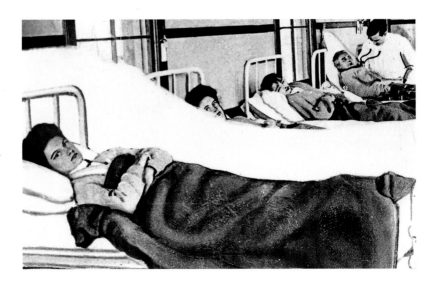

UPTOWN, DOWNTOWN

By 1902, New York City's 3.4 million citizens were no longer well-served by the rackety, sunlight-blocking elevated transit lines (right) that had begun sprouting in the late 1870s. The solution: Follow the example of London (1863), Budapest (1896), Boston (1897) and Paris (1900) by going underground (left). Manhattan's first subway opened in 1904 with a nickel fare. By 1940, there were 462 stations along a 230-mile route (93 miles of it aboveground) crisscrossing every borough.

LEFT: GEORGE P. HALL & SON /
NEW YORK PUBLIC LIBRARY
RIGHT: LEWIS W. HINE /
NEW YORK PUBLIC LIBRARY

AN AGONIZING CHOICE

Panicked seamstresses who escaped burning alive by leaping from 10 stories lay beneath a New York sweat-shop in 1911; the Triangle Shirtwaist Company bolted its exits until quitting time. Of 500 workers (mostly immigrant women aged 13 to 23), 146 perished. Factory owners had to pay 23 families $75 each but were acquitted of manslaughter.

COURTESY OF ILGWU

<

WASTING THEIR YOUTH

Her name is unknown, as is the age of this young cotton spinner from Newton, South Carolina. What is certain: In the 1900s, one-eighth of the South's textile workers were under age 12 (and most tobacco- and cotton-field workers under 10). Industries relying on child labor fended off reforms until 1938 — when unemployed Depression adults coveted those jobs.

LEWIS W. HINE /
NEW YORK PUBLIC LIBRARY

>

THE FORD IN OUR FUTURE

In 1907, he hadn't solved where to put the spare tire (held by a worker at right); yet Henry Ford, 44, was proud to show Detroit the mock-up of his new horse-less buggy. The next year he put the Model T on sale for $825. By the time the Tin Lizzie gave way to the Model A, in 1927, Ford had sold 15 million worldwide — and pioneered modern assembly-line production.

HENRY FORD MUSEUM

The Path Between the Seas

Mariners had long dreamed of channeling through Colombia's narrow Isthmus of Panama to link the Atlantic and Pacific oceans, thereby sparing themselves the 7,000-mile haul around Cape Horn. In the 1800s, a French consortium began digging but ran out of money. In 1902, Teddy Roosevelt petitioned Bogotá to let a U.S. team try. Rebuffed, he encouraged a group of Colombians to form their own country — and then promptly accepted from this new Republic of Panama a sea-to-sea right-of-way in perpetuity. When TR went in 1906 to inspect the Big Ditch (as well as the cab of a steam shovel, above), he became the first sitting president to travel beyond America's borders. The 40-mile-long, 500-foot-wide, 40-foot-deep Panama Canal opened for traffic in 1914 after 10 years; it cost $352 million and some 5,600 lives, mostly victims of tropical diseases.

LEFT: AP
ABOVE: GRANGER COLLECTION

<

THE CRUELEST CONTINENT

A year after America's Robert Peary became the first to stand at the North Pole, a British team under Robert Scott sailed *Terra Nova* to Antarctica hoping to win the race to the South Pole. They reached it on January 18, 1912 — only to find a note left 35 days earlier by Norway's Roald Amundsen. Scott, 44, and his men starved to death on the trek back.

TIME INC.

>

NEW WORLD, NEW LIVES

Bravely emerging from the processing hall at New York's Ellis Island, two tots entered the U.S. Between 1899 to 1907, immigration quadrupled as the vibrant American economy demanded ever more workers. Ellis Island was the main portal because 90 percent of the newcomers sailed from Europe; racially inspired bans on Asians (primarily the Chinese) were lifted only in 1943.

AUGUSTUS FRANCIS SHERMAN /
NEW YORK PUBLIC LIBRARY

>

OTHELLO WITH GLOVES

A black titleholder was unthinkable until Jack Johnson (far right) won the heavyweight crown in 1908, at age 30. Instead of praise, he was reviled for openly courting white women. Ex-champ James Jeffries, 35 (near right), came out of retirement in 1910 to challenge the man he had called a "coon." Bad move: Johnson tattooed him for 14 rounds before dropping him in the 15th.

PHOTOGRAPHER UNKNOWN

25

Tragic Maiden

Since at least the time of Homer, storytellers have preferred tales of adversity and doom. The 20th Century's prime cautionary fable, of course, concerns a state-of-the-art ocean liner and an iceberg. Other shipwrecks have resulted in calamitous losses (the Mississippi side-wheeler *Sultana* burned in 1865, killing 1,500); yet it is RMS *Titanic* that haunts us. Why? Because the disaster contradicts the mantle of techno-infallibility that has defined our age. *This ship is virtually unsinkable*, wrote a trade journal. The claim was echoed by its builders, its owners, its captain, even its awed passengers. Similar boasts have since issued from designers of bridges, zeppelins, space shuttles and PC software. The Greeks had it right: The hardest lesson to learn may be the cost of hubris.

PRIDE OF AN EMPIRE

Towed by tugs to its sea trials on April 2, 1912 (left), *Titanic* was, along with sister ship *Olympic*, the largest liner yet built. England's White Star Line spent some 439 million in today's dollars on each. Promenading passengers (above) who hiked from bow to stern walked 882½ feet — longer, the company's literature boasted, than New York's Woolworth Building, then the world's tallest skyscraper, was high.

TOP LEFT AND ABOVE: TIME INC.

MASTER OF THE SHIP

To mark Captain E.J. Smith's 43 years at sea, White Star gave its retiring top skipper a farewell gift: command of *Titanic*'s first crossing to New York. The ship left port April 10 and soon began picking up radioed warnings of icebergs ahead — including seven on April 14. Yet Smith, 62, never ordered speed to be trimmed.

TIME INC.

THE BUCKLED PLATES

BILGE KEEL

DOUBLE BOTTOM

KEEL

ICE PENETRATING THE DOUBLE BOTTOM

LUXE ON THE HIGH SEAS

The "electrical camel" above was just one amenity of first-class passage ($4,350 for a Parlour Suite; steerage ran from $32). *Titanic* also had a squash court, 30-foot swimming pool, gym and Turkish bath.

BROWN BROTHERS

DEATH OF A LINER

At 2:18 a.m. on April 15, 1912, a shade more than two-and-a-half hours after hitting the iceberg, the bow-flooded *Titanic* began its plunge to the bottom of the North Atlantic. Seven hundred aboard escaped. Fifteen hundred did not.

KEN MARSCHALL /
MADISON PRESS

"ICEBERG RIGHT AHEAD!"

A contemporary British rendition of *Titanic*'s glancing collision with an iceberg also showed the ship's immensity. The top seven of its decks were for passengers, the bottom four levels for machinery, provisions and cargo.

TIME INC.

VALOR AND DISGRACE

When Macy's co-owner Isador Straus, 67, refused a lifeboat seat, so did his wife, Ida, 66. Not all first-class passengers were so gallant. British aristocrat Sir Cosmo Duff Gordon and his wife objected to plucking survivors from the sea, though there was room for 28 more in their 40-person boat.

COURTESY OF STRAUS HISTORICAL SOCIETY

THE FIRST PICTURE SHOW

In 1933's *Cavalcade,* lovers Margaret Lindsay and John Warburton booked passage aboard the you-know-what (note life buoy). Far quicker off the mark were the makers of *Saved from the Titanic*, a silent one-reeler that hit nickelodeons one month after the sinking.

CULVER PICTURES

HE TOLD THE WORLD

Carried off rescue ship *Carpathia* was injured *Titanic* junior telegraphist Harold Bride, 22. He had helped send the standard distress call, CQD, and a new code, SOS. First on land to receive them: New York–based operator David Sarnoff, 21, who in 1926 founded the NBC radio network.

TIME INC.

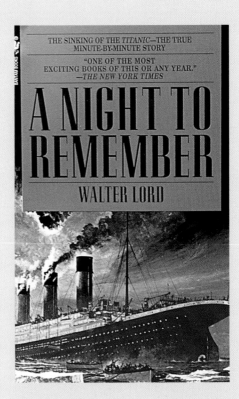

JOHN MEYER

FRESH SEA LEGS

Titanic-mania was reignited in 1955 by veteran journalist Walter Lord's minute-by-minute retelling of
the disaster. The hardcover edition was a best-seller
for six months and the paperback (above) is still in
print. The next year NBC dramatized it in a high-
ratings special; the movie version came out in 1958.

A LIFE UNINTERRUPTED

Before becoming, at 44, *Titanic*'s
most celebrated survivor, Molly
Brown (above) knew both rags and
riches; born to a Missouri ditch-
digger, she headed west and married
a successful gold miner. Her social-
climbing life was memorialized in a
1960 musical that went Hollywood in
1964, with Debbie Reynolds (left) as
The Unsinkable Molly Brown.

ABOVE: COURTESY OF COLORADO
HISTORICAL SOCIETY
LEFT: CULVER PICTURES

LOST AND FOUND

Titanic's remains lay beyond human reach, 2½ miles below the North Atlantic, until 1985. That's when American oceanographer Bob Ballard, 43, and his French partners borrowed experimental deep-sea search gear from the U.S. Navy. Others had mounted high-tech expeditions, but Ballard's was the first to find the liner on the ocean floor, split almost in half lengthwise.

MICHAEL O'NEILL

GRAVE SECRETS

The rust-draped prow (right), as well as the rest of *Titanic*'s exterior sitting atop the muddy seabed, was documented by the Ballard team on videotape and 53,000 stills. Remote-operated cameras also snaked inside the superstructure to capture items like a bathtub (left), dishes and utensils, leather shoes, and a bottle of champagne, cork still intact.

LEFT: WOODS HOLE
RIGHT: EMORY KRISTOF / NGS
IMAGE COLLECTION

STANDING PROWED

Straddling a mock-up of the bow, Leonardo DiCaprio, 23, and Kate Winslet, 22, stirred teenage hearts in 1997's *Titanic*. But their charisma alone could not account for the $1.8 billion worldwide gross of the century's No. 1 blockbuster. Director James Cameron, 43, descended in a Russian submersible to film the wreck. More important, he scripted the affecting love story, and oversaw the special effects, which humanized a night that will long be remembered.

PARAMOUNT PICTURES

HER LIPS ARE SEALED

In 1914, Italian house painter Vincenzo Perugia (above) was convicted of stealing the *Mona Lisa* from Paris's Louvre. It was an open-and-shut case: He was caught trying to fence the 16th Century Da Vinci masterwork. The crime was actually directed by scam artist Eduardo de Valfierno — who didn't even care about the painting. In the two years it was missing, he sold six forgeries, five to nouveau U.S. collectors, at $300,000 per copy. (Louvre officials insist they got back the original.)

LEFT: ERICH LESSING / ART RESOURCE
ABOVE: HARLINQUE COLLECTION

PARIS JEERS A MASTERPIECE

Parisian first-nighters expected the new ballet, created by a trio of fiery Russian émigrés, to be different. Then Igor Stravinsky's dissonant score began, and the curtain rose on wildly costumed members of Serge Diaghilev's troupe executing Vaslav Nijinsky's athletic choreography. The shocked audience jeered loudly enough to drown out the orchestra but not enough to stop the 1913 debut of the modern-dance classic *Sacré du Printemps*, or *Rite of Spring*.

PIERRE BOULAT /
COLLECTION OF BAIER KOCHN

HE WROTE THE SONGS

By 15, the Russian-born orphan of a cantor had quit school and was a singing waiter on New York's Lower East Side. By 19, though unable to read or write music, Irving Berlin was publishing his own songs (which he plunked out on the piano). The first of his 800-plus oeuvre to hit it big was 1911's "Alexander's Ragtime Band." Others: "Blue Skies," "Puttin' on the Ritz," "There's No Business like Show Business," "God Bless America" and one of the top-selling 45s of the century, "White Christmas."

BROWN BROTHERS

REQUIEM

PAUL GAUGUIN
1848–1903

He forfeited, at 35, a career as a stockbroker in Paris to become an Impressionist painter. He then forfeited family and France to move, at 43, to Tahiti. Alas, recognition for his fusing of European technique with native energy — as in the late 1880s self-portrait above — came posthumously.

TIME INC.

MARK TWAIN
1835–1910

On America's centennial he gave the country a charming young hero: Tom Sawyer. Eight years later he created Huck Finn. Samuel Langhorne Clemens of Hannibal, Missouri, was blessed with a vernacularist's ear and a skeptic's eye. He used both to become a master storyteller.

TIME INC.

HARRIET TUBMAN
1821–1913

Born on a Maryland plantation into slavery, she fled north in 1849. Yet Tubman kept going home to help other blacks (among them, her parents) board the Underground Railroad to free states or Canada. And during the Civil War, she posed as a menial in her native South to spy for the Union.

LIBRARY OF CONGRESS

<
GERONIMO
1829–1909

Broken treaties consigned his Chiricahua Apaches to a corner of Arizona with neither water nor game, so Geronimo led one of the West's last major Indian uprisings, finally surrendering in 1886. A rebel with a cause? Yes. But he was a guest of honor at Theodore Roosevelt's 1905 inauguration — and ended his days as a farmer in Oklahoma.

CORBIS / BETTMANN

>
LEO TOLSTOY
1828–1910

By age 50, he had published two canons of Western literature: *War and Peace* and *Anna Karenina.* Then the Russian nobleman took up religious asceticism and renounced his land and earthly goods. Although estranged, his family all hurried to the remote town of Astapova to be at his bedside when he succumbed to pneumonia.

TIME INC.

<
HENRIK IBSEN
1828–1906

Between 1879 and 1890, his country's greatest playwright crafted three social dramas so timeless they still need no updating: *A Doll's House*, *An Enemy of the People* and *Hedda Gabler.* But they were written abroad. A commercial and artistic flop at home, Ibsen spent his most productive years in Italy and Germany before returning to Norway.

ROYAL MINISTRY OF FOREIGN AFFAIRS, PRESS AND CULTURAL RELATIONS DEPARTMENT, OSLO

FREDERIC REMINGTON
1861–1909

Born in upstate New York, this Yalie (he attended the college's art school) went west to become America's best-known interpreter of the vanishing cowboy life. Whether in magazine illustrations, oil paintings or, most famously, his visceral bronzes, Remington's celebrations of frontier machismo were anything but tenderfooted.

FREDERIC REMINGTON MUSEUM

SUSAN B. ANTHONY
1820–1906

Angry that her teaching pay was one-fifth a male's, she protested by quitting and joining the temperance movement. Then, at 32, Anthony began to champion female suffrage. U.S. women would not get to vote in a national election until 1920. But for her groundbreaking crusade Anthony was, in 1979, the first native-born woman to be commemorated on an American coin.

FLORENCE NIGHTINGALE
1820–1910

She led 38 nurses to the Crimea in 1854 to tend wounded troops, only to be cursed by British army doctors for her meddling. But the men adored their "Lady of the Lamp" for making nightly rounds; she sailed home a hero. Nightingale founded the world's first school of nursing in 1860 and in 1907 became the first woman honored with Britain's Order of Merit.

CAMERA PRESS

CASEY JONES
1864–1900

The Illinois Central engineer in the cab was known for a heavy hand on the throttle, so naturally his *Cannonball* express was steaming full tilt. Near Vaughan, Mississippi, he was warned that the track was blocked. Ordering his fireman to jump, he hit the brakes. Passengers and crew walked away but not the man whose heroics are retold in the ballad "Casey Jones."

ILLINOIS CENTRAL RAILROAD

HENRY MORTON STANLEY
1841–1904

Arriving in the U.S. at 18, the Welsh bastard John Rowland took a new name and became a reporter. In 1869, the New York *Herald* sent Stanley after a Scottish explorer who had vanished in Africa while searching for the headwaters of the Nile. Two years later, in what is currently Tanzania, his hunt ended with "Dr. Livingstone, I presume?"

TIME INC.

The tanks, the troops, the caissons, the cavalry, the
supply wagons: American. The place: France. The year:
1917. The enemy: somewhere beyond the horizon.

1914–1919

THE WAR TO END ALL WARS

Victory Proved Easier Than Peace

BY DAVID M. KENNEDY

T 8:20 ON THE evening of April 2, 1917, President Woodrow Wilson left the White House, stepped into a waiting automobile and motored through the rain up Pennsylvania Avenue toward Capitol Hill accompanied by a clattering troop of cavalry that cantered alongside his car. Minutes later, after composing himself briefly in a Capitol anteroom, the President strode through the swinging doors of the House chamber to face an extraordinary joint session of Congress. The packed hall erupted in emotional applause, but Wilson's manner was solemn and burdened. For only the fourth time in American history, a president was about to ask Congress for a formal declaration of war.

The Imperial German government, Wilson explained, desperate to bring its adversaries in the three-year-old European War to their knees, had for the last two months been violating international law by waging unrestricted submarine warfare against neutral shipping bound for Britain and France. "American ships have been sunk, American lives taken," said Wilson, and the United States had no choice but to "accept the status

of belligerent which has thus been thrust upon it." Four days later, with 50 dissenting votes in the House and six in the Senate, Congress granted Wilson's request. The United States had now entered the Great War.

"It is a fearful thing to lead this great peaceful people into war, into the most terrible and disastrous of all wars," Wilson said. Fearful indeed. Since the bark of Gavrilo Princip's pistol in Sarajevo on June 28, 1914, had shattered the peace of the Old World, millions of young Europeans had perished. In the east, the Czar's armies had absorbed more than one million casualties in the war's first year alone. Russian officers then resorted to herding unarmed peasants into battle and certain slaughter —

helping to kindle the seething popular resentments that would soon revolutionize Russia and extinguish the Romanov dynasty. On the western front, once the scything sweep of the German armies had been stopped at the River Marne in September 1914,

He fought out West (with a Negro unit, thus the nickname Black Jack), in Cuba, in the Philippines, in Manchuria, in Mexico. At 56, John J. Pershing was ready to shape an American Expeditionary Force and lead it to France in 1917 to fight alongside the Allies.

the fighting had congealed into the grisly and prodigiously bloody stalemate of trench warfare. The five-month-long siege of Verdun in 1916 butchered more than 300,000 Germans and an equal number of Frenchmen. A single battle along the Somme River in the same year killed 420,000 Britons; a year later another 245,000 died at Passchendaele.

To a degree that later generations would find baffling, some young American men — especially if they were well educated — greeted Wilson's war message with unbridled enthusiasm and uncritical patriotic fervor. William Langer, later a distinguished Harvard historian, recalled with some perplexity his generation's "eagerness to get to France and above all to see the front."

One would think that after almost four years of war, after the most detailed and realistic accounts of murderous fighting on the Somme and around Verdun, to say nothing of the day-to-day agony of trench warfare, it would have been all but impossible to get anyone to serve without duress. But . . . we men, most of us young, were simply fascinated by the prospect of adventure and heroism. Most of us, I think, had the feeling that life, if we survived, would run in the familiar, routine channel. Here was our one great chance for excitement and risk. We could not afford to pass it up.

Similarly, the 1916 Harvard graduate and future novelist John Dos Passos recollected that "we had spent our boyhood in the afterglow of the peaceful nineteenth century. . . . What was war like? We wanted to see with our own eyes. We flocked into the volunteer services. I respected the conscientious objectors, and occasionally felt that I should take that course myself, but hell, I wanted to see the show."

Harvard men may have volunteered, but the vast American Expeditionary Force (AEF) hastily mobilized in 1917–1918 was mostly built with conscripts. Their army mirrored the predominantly rural, sur-

prisingly backward and astonishingly polyglot society from which they were ladled. A farmer from Jackson County, Missouri, Captain Harry S Truman exemplified the agrarian background of a majority of World War I American servicemen. Yet in other ways he was an unusual doughboy. At five feet eight inches in height, Truman stood a full inch taller than the average recruit. As a high school graduate, he had almost twice as many years of schooling as the typical native-born white draftee, three times more than immigrant conscripts and four times more than most black soldiers, who were mustered into segregated units and assigned almost exclusively to noncombat duty. Some 25 percent of all draftees were illiterate; few had any knowledge of the world beyond their town or neighborhood or, more typically, beyond their isolated rural county or even beyond the farthest furrow of their own farm.

Truman was also an old-stock American, while one in five draftees had been born abroad. They were the children of the great European diaspora that had brought more than 17 million migrants to American shores in the quarter century before the war's outbreak. The AEF's censors had to scan letters penned in 49 languages. A wartime joke had it that when one officer called his unit's roll, not a single soldier recognized the pronunciation of his name; but when the officer sneezed, 10 men stepped forward.

Among the reasons Wilson had hesitated for so long to lead his country into the war was his anxiety about the loyalties of those great immigrant communities. One in every three Americans was foreign-born in 1914 or had at least one foreign-born parent; more than 10 million of them came from Germany or from Germany's ally, Austria-Hungary. They were freshly arrived and still largely unacclimated; indeed, many had not yet committed themselves to remaining permanently in America. Most men will fight for their country, Mark Twain once remarked, but few will fight for their boarding-

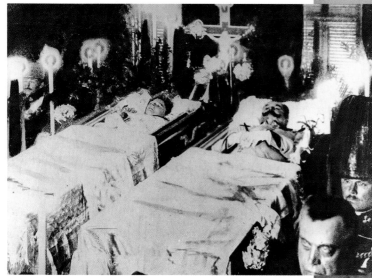

SETTING FLAME TO TINDER

Europe had enjoyed an uneasy peace for 44 years when on June 28, 1914, Archduke Franz Ferdinand (top), heir to the Austro-Hungarian Empire, left city hall in Sarajevo, provincial capital of Bosnia and Herzegovina, with his wife. Their car was just under way when Serbian nationalist Gavrilo Princip, 19, began shooting; Duchess Sophie was 46, the archduke 50. In less than 10 weeks, nine nations had mobilized and launched the Great War.

TIME INC. (2)

AN ARMY IS BLOODED

Some 30,000 British troops had just arrived to defend Mons, a dreary Belgian mining town when, on August 23, 1914, the Germans attacked, 160,000 strong. The British held — but not the large French force on their right flank. Retreat was sounded. The Germans followed deep into France. Thoughts of a quick Allied triumph vanished.

TIME INC.

THE WAITING GAME

Trench warfare, directed from underground bunkers like this French command post, soon came to characterize the combat between the vast but immobile armies of the Allies and the Central Powers. Valiant charges "over the top" into hostile fire resulted in nightmarish casualties but little territory gained. Both sides adopted the same strategy: victory through attrition.

TIME INC.

ROAD TO NOWHERE

The jauntiness with which British troops had steamed across the English Channel to take on the Hun faded on the killing fields of France. Between 1914 and 1919, 6.2 million Englishmen were mobilized (out of an adult male population of 20.5 million). More than 744,000 did not make it home.

TIME INC.

ST. PETERSBURG RULES

All was mercifully quiet on the eastern front for Russian officers guarding the Carpathians, the mountains between their motherland and Hungary. Manpower was not an issue — in 1914, after 125,000 Russians were captured by the Germans at Tannenberg, Czar Nicholas II just ordered more serfs drafted — but firepower was: One-third of the men lacked guns. By the end of the war, Russia's dead, wounded or captured exceeded nine million troops.

<

AN INVASION BLUNTED

One month after the first guns sounded in August of 1914, German troops (here using a parish church as a hospital) had pushed to within 25 miles of Paris. Overconfident generals thereupon sent two corps east to fight Russia — only to see their drawn-down forces checked by the French and the British at the River Marne. The Germans were still stuck there when the second battle of Marne was waged four years later.

TIME INC.

>

BOTCHED CHANCE

The goal: Land 75,000 British, Australian and New Zealand troops on Turkey's Mediterranean coast and drive up the Gallipoli Peninsula to Istanbul, seat of the Ottoman Empire. The April 1915 invasion went well — but then Commonwealth leaders chose to slow their advance. The Turks rallied. By mid-May, 25,000 Allies were dead or wounded; by year's end, the surviving troops were evacuated.

TIME INC.

REVENGE FOR FERDINAND

A Serb assassinated their archduke, so Austro-Hungarian soldiers had no qualms about executing Serbian POWs. The violence spread geographically too. In 1915, Italy and Bulgaria ended their neutrality, raising to 11 the number of warring nations.

NATIONAL ARCHIVES

I DREAMED I SAW . . .

. . . Joe Hill on almost his last night, in Salt Lake City, where the Swedish-born labor organizer and troubadour awaited death by firing squad in 1915. He had been convicted of a double killing on evidence so flimsy even President Wilson protested. Brash to the end, Hill, 36, asked to be buried elsewhere: "I don't want to be found dead in Utah."

CORBIS / BETTMANN

PLANNING PARENTHOOD

Twice in 1916 Margaret Sanger landed in New York courts for preaching contraception. First the ex-nurse, 36, was charged with obscenity for mailing pamphlets that described techniques; the case was dismissed. Later she drew 30 days for opening, in Brooklyn, the nation's first clinic to advise on birth control (a term coined by Sanger).

CORBIS / BETTMANN-UPI

RUE, BRITANNIA

On Easter Monday, 1916, Dublin's tranquillity was broken when Irish nationalists seized key sites to protest British rule. The empire struck back, shelling the main post office (left) and forcing a quick surrender. The British then executed 15 leaders of the uprising. That blunder aroused dormant patriotism and led to the 1922 creation of the predominantly Catholic state now known as the Republic of Ireland.

TIME INC.

ACROSS THE RIO GRANDE

The last foreign troops to invade the Lower 48 were led by Mexico's Pancho Villa. After helping oust the dictators Porfirio Díaz and Victoriano Huerta, he fell out with fellow insurgents. In 1916, Villa, 38, and his loyalists shot up Columbus, New Mexico. John Pershing and 4,000 U.S. soldiers chased him for a year across northern Mexico in vain.

TIME INC.

Enter Singing

In 1900, in an unruly part of Manhattan's West Side, impresarios were building theaters to hold a stupefying 1,500. For years, minstrels and vaudevillians had taken their acts to the remotest burgs. Now the best found a home on Broadway. In this Great White hothouse, melodists and bards joined to beget a uniquely American art form, in which songs, and later dance, advanced the story — a formula copied worldwide. Rival mass entertainments soon emerged. Nickelodeons grew into Hollywood, radio into TV, sports into neo-religion. Broadway (whose biggest house still holds just 1,933) has often read its own closing notice. Each has been premature.

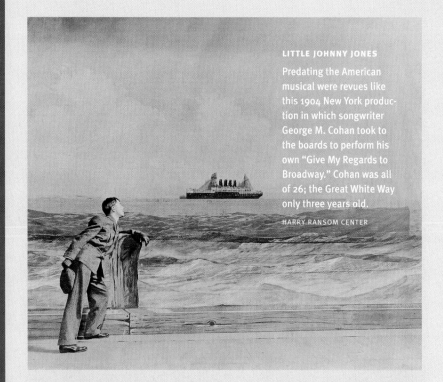

LITTLE JOHNNY JONES
Predating the American musical were revues like this 1904 New York production in which songwriter George M. Cohan took to the boards to perform his own "Give My Regards to Broadway." Cohan was all of 26; the Great White Way only three years old.
HARRY RANSOM CENTER

VERY GOOD EDDIE
Jerome Kern and Guy Bolton created, in 1915, a show with one plot, two acts and, most important, seven songs that advanced the story. The first American musical told of the confusion that beset two honeymooning couples. Among those who saw it: a teenage aspiring composer named Richard Rodgers.
HARRY RANSOM CENTER

SHOW BOAT
Novelist Edna Ferber's 1926 best-seller was about entertainers who plied the Mississippi in a paddle wheeler. Jerome Kern and lyricist Oscar Hammerstein II took 14 months to craft from it a drama laced with complex social issues — a first on Broadway — and a score that, like "Ol' Man River," jus' keeps rollin' along.
ROGERS AND HAMMERSTEIN ORGANIZATION

Pittsburgh native Gene Kelly broke through in a 1940 musical by Richard Rodgers and Lorenz Hart that married, as never before, story (or "book") and music. More audacious yet was the plot, drawn from a set of John O'Hara stories: Kelly, 28, portrayed a sleazy rake. The dark play bewitched audiences even as it left them bothered and bewildered.

RALPH MORSE / LIFE

OKLAHOMA!

Sure, the corn was as
high as a elephant's eye.
But to a nation gone from
Depression to war, this first
tuneful collaboration of
Rodgers and Hammerstein,
in 1943, was like a wind
sweepin' down the plain.
Based on the play *Green
Grow the Lilacs*, it was
the first musical to use
choreography (by the
ballet-trained Agnes de
Mille) to advance the story.

GJON MILI / LIFE

SOUTH PACIFIC

War memories were still fresh when Mary Martin, 34, leaped to stardom in 1949 as a Navy nurse in the Pacific. The bittersweet Rodgers and Hammerstein show, based on James Michener's tales, was disturbingly topical (pointing out that even in paradise there was racism). And in a steal from Hollywood, the orchestra played beneath the dialogue.

PHILIPPE HALSMAN

MY FAIR LADY

George Bernard Shaw's 1913 stage hit, *Pygmalion*, had stumped all attempts at musicalization until Frederick Loewe and Alan Jay Lerner took a shot. Their 1956 show — seamlessly melding book and song — starred Rex Harrison (above, right) and an ingenue with a four-octave voice, Julie Andrews, 20.

LEONARD MCCOMBE / LIFE

WEST SIDE STORY

From Romeo and Juliet to Tony and Maria? Composer Leonard Bernstein and choreographer Jerome Robbins originally planned an innovative, dance-driven update of Shakespeare set on New York's turn-of-the-century Lower East Side. By 1957, the other side of town was hotter, and whites versus Puerto Ricans had supplanted Catholics versus Jews. Only in America. . . .

HANK WALKER / LIFE

HAIR

Wasn't 1967 about time for baby boomers to see their (counter)culture take center stage? Well, good morning, sunshine.... Gerome Ragni and James Rado set the karma from that year's "Summer of Love" against the increasingly bad vibes from a place called Nam. And for their "American tribal love-rock musical," they picked a title sure to rile the geezers.

RALPH MORSE / LIFE

A CHORUS LINE

In a drafty rehearsal hall, gypsy dancers like Pamela Blair confided their showbiz dreams while trying out for bit parts in a Broadway extravaganza. The Michael Bennett–Marvin Hamlisch show, as austere as the traditional musical was gaudy, opened in 1975 and ran for a then-record 15 years.

MARTHA SWOPE / TIME INC.

> **AIN'T MISBEHAVIN'**

Sixty-five years after black musical revues were consigned uptown to Harlem, Broadway decided the most important color was green. Richard Maltby Jr.'s ground-breaking 1978 tribute to the ebullient pianist-composer Fats Waller sparked a run of hits that mined black song and dance, among them *Jelly's Last Jam* and *Bring in da Noise, Bring in da Funk*.

MARTHA SWOPE / TIME INC.

< **FOLLIES**

Nobody had accused Broadway of being too cerebral — until 1971, when in rode Gene Nelson. The vehicle, courtesy of Stephen Sondheim and Harold Prince, probed the memories of two aging Ziegfeld girls by way of a nonlinear (and virtually nonexistent) plot. The "concept musical" proved a format that few besides Sondheim could adroitly handle.

MARTHA SWOPE / TIME INC.

> **RENT**

Broadway was ruled by the British megahits of Lloyd Webber and by pricey revivals when Jonathan Larson arrived in 1996. His protean rock opera reset Puccini's *La Bohème* in New York's East Village and fused a cornucopia of musical genres: electric rock, Motown, reggae, salsa, even gospel. Three weeks before opening night, Larson died unexpectedly of an aortic aneurysm; he was 35.

JOAN MARCUS

TEN DAYS THAT SHOOK THE WORLD

In early 1917, with their country's scant food
and fuel diverted to a futile war, Russians
began to riot, most notably in the newly
renamed capital of Petrograd (above). The czar
had barely survived an uprising in 1905. Now
Nicholas abdicated. A provisional government
soon fell to the Reds (Communists), who were
counterattacked by the Whites (the czar's
loyalists). The Russian Revolution was on.

TIME INC.

A MASSACRE — AND A MYSTERY

The imminent turmoil seemed not to faze Nicholas (above, center, with heir apparent Prince Alexis, 14; his four daughters, ages 17 to 23; and palace guards). The imperial family soon surrendered to the Reds and was taken to an estate in the Ural mountains to await a show trial. But on July 16, 1918, as the White Army neared, the czar and czarina, the five young Romanovs, plus four servants were slain with guns and bayonets. The 11 corpses were removed from the bullet-pocked room (left), doused with acid and tossed in an unmarked grave. Yet Soviet officials exhuming the remains in 1991 found only nine bodies.

ABOVE AND LEFT: TIME INC.

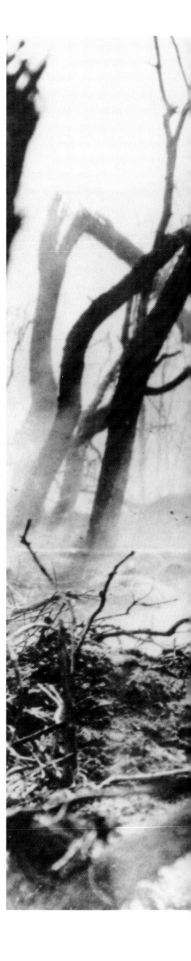

<

THE YANKS ARE COMING

Private T.P. Laughlin of the New York National Guard said goodbye in 1917 after being called to active duty. Reacting in part to German submarine attacks on U.S. merchant ships, America ended its neutrality despite having an army with fewer than 130,000 men. But the first doughboys (slang for troops since Custer's time) were in France by June and in combat by October.

NATIONAL ARCHIVES

NEXT, THE RHINE

American troops mounted their first major offensive in September 1918, 15 months after the Yank vanguard reached France. The battle-field — Saint-Mihiel, in German hands for four years. Aided by thick fog, the U.S. First Army, now 1.4 million men strong, punched through. It then joined with French forces to win back the Argonne Forest. The German retreat was under way.

U.S. SIGNAL CORPS

<

A DEADLY DEVELOPMENT

Two U.S. Signal Corpsmen were braced for a weapon new to World War I: poison gas. Though the 1899 Hague Convention banned chemical warfare, Germany began using gas in 1915. At first, Allied and German soldiers alike (the yellow clouds turned with the wind) had no protection beyond a wet hankie. It took a year to develop a working mask.

CULVER PICTURES

FREE AT LAST

The 369th Infantry was rightly jubilant sailing back to New York in 1919. Three-quarters of the 200,000 black men in uniform served as menials or musicians — black women seeking to be nurses were rejected out of hand — but the 369th was different. The Harlem Hellfighters not only went toe-to-toe with Jerry but also became the first U.S. unit to reach the Rhine.

NATIONAL ARCHIVES

>

HOME IS THE HERO

Safely back in Tennessee, Alvin York, 32, showed Mom his Medal of Honor and Croix de Guerre. In 1918's Meuse-Argonne campaign, the blacksmith, denied conscientious-objector status, charged a German machine-gun nest alone. He killed 25 and captured the rest; then, returning to HQ, York accepted more surrenders. Total POWs he delivered that day: 132.

VITAGRAPH, INC.

A FAREWELL TO ARMS

Were these troops happy to leave their New Jersey demobilization center in late 1918? More so than the four-legged souvenir of war clutched by the doughboy on the running board. All told, 2.1 million Yanks went Over There. Some 122,500 ended up in graves or missing; another 237,135 returned wounded.

NATIONAL ARCHIVES

DIAMOND SCANDAL

In 1919, Joe Jackson, 31, had another All-Star year (.351 average, 96 RBIs) to lead his White Sox to the World Series. But when the underdog Cincinnati Reds won, he and seven teammates were charged with fixing the outcome on behalf of gamblers. Shoeless Joe said it wasn't so, and the jury agreed. But baseball banned him and the rest of the Chicago Black Sox for life.

CORBIS / BETTMANN

INVISIBLE ENEMIES

Near war's end, two fevers swept America. Seattle cops wore masks in 1918 to guard against Spanish flu, a strain targeting those aged 20 to 40. Borne across oceans by transiting soldiers, it killed a half million in the United States, 20 million worldwide. The other virus — the Red Menace of Bolshevism — would take far longer to run its course.

NATIONAL ARCHIVES

RUSSIA TURNS RED

Two years earlier, this 49-year-old revolutionary preaching communism in Moscow's newly renamed Red Square was sneaking back to Mother Russia inside a boxcar. Czar Nicholas had vacated his throne — and in chaos, Vladimir I. Lenin saw opportunity. Rightly so. By 1919, the civil war had been won, and power cemented, by his Bolsheviks.

TIME INC.

WAS THIS TRIP NECESSARY?

They rolled out the carpet for Woodrow Wilson in Dover, England, one month after the armistice ending World War I. The president, 61, was sailing to peace talks in France. He would play a pivotal role in forging the Treaty of Versailles. Congress, blind to issues beyond America's borders, rejected not only the pact but also U.S. membership in the League of Nations.

NATIONAL ARCHIVES

TURNING POINT:
CLOSING THE GENDER GAP

You Go, Girl!

The Founding Fathers didn't specifically preclude the Founding Mothers from a role in democracy. No need to: During the republic's early years, women largely endured second-class citizenship, a bias inherited from millennia of Western culture. Things began to change with the opening of the American West. On the frontier, gender counted for less than can-do spirit. By the late 19th Century, many states had rewritten laws allowing women to own property. Yet calls by early suffragettes for voting rights were met with hoots; in 1900, women could cast ballots in a national election only in New Zealand. World War I helped tip the scales in America (see pages 64–65). At century's end, women have achieved every major elected and appointed post in the country except the two highest. Can't stop thinking about tomorrow. . . .

(see pages 64–65)

ONE WOMAN, ONE VOTE

On August 20, 1920, when Tennessee became the required 36th state to ratify the 19th Amendment into law, Alice Paul lifted a glass (of grape juice, thanks to the 18th Amendment). The militant Paul, 35, didn't quit there. She later helped lobby gender-equality passages into the U.N. charter and the U.S. Civil Rights Act of 1964.

CORBIS / BETTMAN-UPI

PUBLIC NUISANCES

New York mayor George B. McClellan was no doubt unavailable when suffragettes called on City Hall in 1908; police officers made sure the ladies didn't linger. Things were better out West. Wyoming entered the Union in 1890 with the first constitution to grant women the vote in state and local elections.

CULVER PICTURES

<

IS ANYONE LISTENING?

The marchers' blunt message was true until 1917, when their state joined 14 others (out of 48) in granting women at least some voting rights. The U.S. House voted in 1918 to make it the law of the land, but Southern senators balked at enfranchising black women. Congress finally passed the 19th Amendment the next year.

CULVER PICTURES

>

USE IT OR LOSE IT

Members of the brand-new League of Women Voters prepared to entrain for the 1920 Democratic Convention in San Francisco. The organization, called the National American Woman Suffrage Association until the 19th Amendment was ratified, began life with an impressive two million members.

ARCHIVE PHOTOS

PEACE IN HER TIME

The first U.S. congress-woman (representing her native Montana) could vote for herself in 1916 but not for a presidential candidate. Jeannette Rankin lost her next run after opposing America's entry into World War I. Her continued paci-fism (above, in 1932, at age 51) led to a second term in 1940; she thereupon be-came the lone legislator to vote against declaring war on Japan after Pearl Harbor.

AP

A PIONEER APPOINTEE

The 1933 Senate confirmation of Frances Perkins, 51, as Secretary of Labor made her the first female cabinet member. Though thought "soft" by both industry and labor, she helped craft New Deal laws on unemployment compen-sation, minimum wage, maximum workweek and Social Security. Perkins resigned in 1945, two months after the death of her mentor, FDR.

AP

WELCOME TO "THE CLUB"

Exultant four-term representative Margaret Chase Smith, 52, of Maine won the GOP nomination for the Senate in 1948. By then capturing the election, she became the first woman to sit in both houses of Congress. Smith, whom Eisenhower considered for veep in 1952 before choosing Richard Nixon, served four terms in the Senate.

CORBIS / BETTMANN-ACME

DON'T FENCE HER IN

"Unbought and unbossed" was the slogan of Brooklyn's Shirley Chisholm, who in 1968, at 43, became the first black congresswoman. She proved just as feisty on the Hill. Named to a subcommittee overseeing forestry, Chisholm asked aloud if that was because House leaders knew little about her home borough except that "a tree grew there." They caved. She won reelection six times.

FRED DE VAN

THE RISING SUN

Japan's 124th emperor — Hirohito, installed in 1926 at age 25 — named his reign Showa, or Enlightened Peace. But over the next decade he did little to curb his nation's military adventures in China. Nor, as he was about to mark his 15th anniversary on the throne, did Hirohito balk at plans for an air attack on an American naval base at Pearl Harbor, Hawaii.

TIME INC.

A SOUND BARRIER FALLS

"You ain't heard nothin' yet!" bragged Al Jolson, segueing into "Toot, Toot, Tootsie!" Audiences for 1927's *The Jazz Singer* flipped over the first movie with synchronized speech. Jolson, 41 (above, with Eugenie Besserer and Warner Oland), played a cantor's son torn between religion and showbiz. Unlike many silent-era stars, he would thrive in the talkies.

FRANK DRIGGS COLLECTION

DARWIN ON TRIAL

At 65, his three runs for the White House long past, William Jennings Bryan (right) agreed in 1925 to help the state of Tennessee prosecute John T. Scopes, 24, for teaching evolution. Opposing counsel Clarence Darrow called on Bryan to defend the Bible's version of creation. He could not. Five days after Scopes was found guilty (a verdict later overturned), Bryan died of a heart attack.

CORBIS / BETTMANN-UPI

HITLER DOES TIME

His 1923 coup against the government of Bavaria a flop, Adolf Hitler, 34 (near right), had to serve eight soft months at Landsberg Fortress. Among his visitors: Rudolf Hess (in tan suit), to whom Hitler dictated *Revenge*, the first half of *Mein Kampf (My Struggles)*, his best-selling encomium to Aryan superiority.

TIME INC.

REVOLUTIONARY EPIC

Sergei Eisenstein, 27, had directed only one feature when Moscow asked him to make a film marking the 20th anniversary of the abortive 1905 uprising against the czar. He delivered *Potemkin* — and forever altered cinema. Eisenstein's tale of mutiny aboard a battleship docked at Odessa was driven by rapid-fire montages. Many have copied the device; few have employed it better.

MOVIE STILL ARCHIVES

THE LONE EAGLE

The prize for the first nonstop flight from New York to Paris: $25,000. On May 21, 1927, airmail pilot Charles Lindbergh, 25, not only claimed the money by flying the 3,610 miles in 33½ hours but also became a worldwide celebrity for doing it solo. After hopping over to England (top right) in *Spirit of St. Louis*, where thousands cheered, he returned to America. By ship.

RIGHT: TIME INC.
BELOW RIGHT: CULVER PICTURES

THOSE LIPS, THOSE EYES

He emigrated from Italy at 18 to work as a laborer, broke into movies at 23 — and wound up Hollywood's first hunk. Rudolf Valentino never got to see if his smoldering eroticism *(The Sheik, Blood and Sand)* would play in the sound era; he died in 1926, at 31, of a perforated ulcer. Thirty thousand women, led by first wife Jean Acker (far right), mobbed the funeral home.

ABOVE: TIME INC.
RIGHT: ARCHIVE PHOTOS

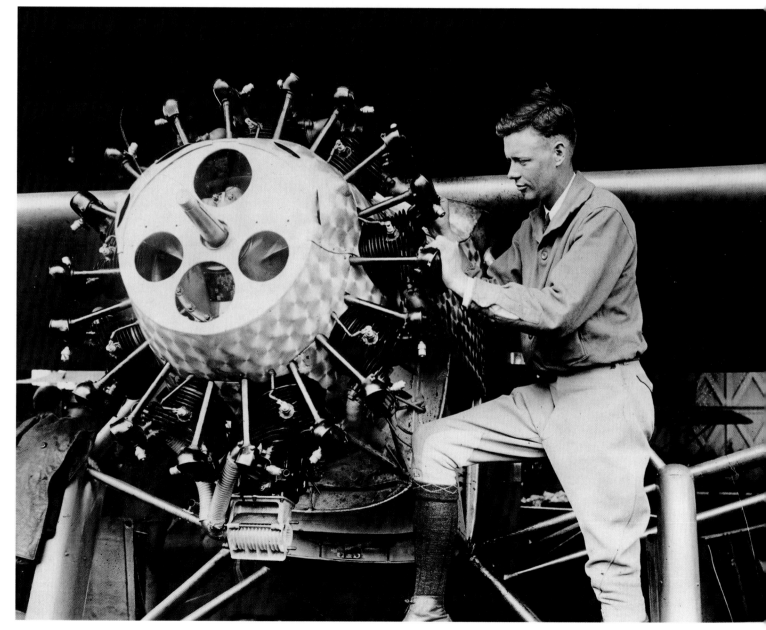

LET THE GAMES BEGIN

When his pay hit $80,000, George Herman Ruth was asked why he merited a salary larger than President Hoover's. Cracked the Babe, or so it was reported, "I'm having a better year." Before World War I, the most renowned and rewarded athletes were boxers, whose prizefights were described in every newspaper. Then came the infant but insistent medium of radio. How to fill hour upon hour of empty airtime? Well, sporting events were cheap to broadcast. An America flush with leisure time and pocket cash responded, transforming mere diversion into an industry. The Twenties were a time for heroes to emerge and profit. Some, like the Babe, did.

<
SWIMMING TO TINSELTOWN
Romanian-born, Chicago-reared Johnny Weissmuller quit ninth grade to focus on swimming. In addition to setting 67 world marks, he won three Olympic golds in 1924 and a pair more in 1928. Weissmuller then went Hollywood and vine, playing Tarzan 12 times before ending his acting career as big- and small-screen hero Jungle Jim.

JANZTEN, INC.

GOING, GOING, GONE...
The Baby Ruth candy bar was in fact named for President Cleveland's infant daughter. All other tales about the Yankee slugger are true. He played hard, lived harder. More to the point, by repeatedly swatting the new "live" ball over fences — 60 times in 1927, 714 times in a 21-year career — Babe Ruth helped his sport escape the long shadow of its 1919 Black Sox scandal.

CORBIS / BETTMANN-UPI
<

>
DESPERATION PLAY
It was third-and-long for the five-year-old, 13-team National Football League when the Chicago Bears paid an All-America halfback from the University of Illinois $100,000 to turn pro. Red Grange (with ball) earned every dime. In 1925, the Galloping Ghost packed the house for 18 games, including exhibitions, and made the NFL viable.

CORBIS / BETTMANN-INP

TWO TENNIS TERRORS

There was no country-club politeness about the games of Helen Wills and Bill Tilden: Each crushed foes with raw power. Wills won her first U.S. Open in 1923, at 18, and added six Opens and eight Wimbledons over the next 15 years. From 1927 to 1932, she lost not one set of singles. Tilden was almost as dominant, capturing seven U.S. and three Wimbledon titles between 1920 and 1930. But his fortunes declined after he retired in 1937, at 44. Back then, his homo-sexuality was little tolerated: Tilden died in 1953, poor and alone.

TOP LEFT: CULVER PICTURES
TOP RIGHT: CORBIS /
BETTMANN-ACME

LET THE GAMES BEGIN

THEY SWAPPED LEATHER

Jack Dempsey (above) was 24 when he rode a string of savage KOs to the heavy-weight championship in 1919. Called the Manassa Mauler, he kept the crown until 1926, when ex-Marine Gene Tunney, 29, took it away. Their rematch the next year became the most controversial bout in ring history. Dempsey battered Tunney to the canvas but was slow to move to a neutral corner. The delay gave his foe more than 10 seconds to recover; aided by the "long count," Tunney won the fight.

ABOVE AND TOP RIGHT:
CULVER PICTURES

A CHANNEL CROSSING

Two years after winning a gold and a pair of bronzes at the 1924 Paris Olympics, Manhattan-born Gertrude Ederle, 19, became the sixth person — and first woman — to swim the English Channel. Her time for the grueling 35 miles was the fastest yet by nearly two hours. But Ederle's 14½-hour effort aggravated an ear problem that later rendered her deaf.

CULVER PICTURES

THE ICE PRINCESS

Figure skating was as dull as a compulsory figure eight until Sonja Henie. The Norwegian used her ballet training to create fluid and exciting freestyle programs; at 15 she won the first of 10 straight world titles, to which she added three Olympic golds. Henie went on to star in an ice revue and a dozen lame but popular movies (e.g., *Sun Valley Serenade*).

CORBIS / BETTMANN-UPI

FIRING AT THE PIN

It wasn't his exquisite game that made Bobby Jones an idol nor his run of 13 major titles in eight years. Instead, it was the wonder of an amateur (and full-time lawyer) repeatedly besting the top pros. After winning the Grand Slam in 1930, Jones, 28, withdrew from competitive golf to help found and nurture the Masters tournament in his native Georgia.

HUTLON DEUTSCH / LIAISON

THE ORIGINAL WORLD OF DISNEY

In 1926, animator Walt Disney, 25 (fourth from left), posed with his entire staff and Margie Gay, the star of his *Alice in Cartoonland* series. At the time, Disney's studio was rodentless — and struggling. Two years later, however, along came *Steamboat Willie* and a mouse named Mickey (whose pip-squeak voice was provided by Walt himself).

PHOTOGRAPHER UNKNOWN

YOU LIKE ME! YOU REALLY LIKE ME!

First time around, they just ate and drank; this time they also gave out gilded statuettes. Winners included *Wings* (best production), Emil Jannings (best actor) and Janet Gaynor (best actress). In 1931, the statuette was dubbed Oscar. In 1943, they cut out the food and wine. In 1953, the rest of us got to tune in and giggle through the acceptance speeches.

ACADEMY OF MOTION PICTURE ARTS & SCIENCES

HOW TO DRIVE OVER WATER

When work began on the George Washington Bridge in 1927, New York City was accessible to those west of the Hudson only by train and ferry. The 3,500-foot span was the world's longest suspension bridge from its 1931 ribbon cutting until San Francisco opened its Golden Gate Bridge in 1936.

FELIKS DZERZHINSKY
1877–1926

The Polish-born socialist joined Russia's anticzarist Bolsheviks and, with their triumph in 1917, won a key post: internal security. Cheka, the ruthless secret police he founded, would later go by OGPU, NKVD and KGB. Fittingly, Lubyan-ka, the notorious prison in Moscow where "enemies of the state" were tortured, sat on Dzerzhinsky Square.

TIME INC.

<

JOSEPH CONRAD
1857–1924

Two decades at sea gave the son of a Polish patriot exotic settings for novels that relentlessly explore the corrosive impact of greed and corruption. Conrad Anglicized his name and wrote — in English — *Heart of Darkness*, *Nostromo* and *The Secret Agent*. Yet shortly before his death, the naturalized British subject refused knighthood.

CORBIS / BETTMANN

>

ALEXANDER GRAHAM BELL
1847–1922

Teaching elocution to the hearing impaired led the audiologist to experiment with the electric transmis-sion of sound. While the telephone, invented when he was 29, could not help his favorite deaf pupil, Mabel Hubbard, she mar-ried him anyway. Bell also devised a kite to carry people and bred sheep more likely to bear twins.

TIME INC.

FRANZ KAFKA
1883–1924

An assimilated German Jew
who was both a distinct
minority in his native
Prague and a misfit within
his family, Kafka supported
himself as a lawyer. Nights
were spent crafting grimly
humorous fiction like *The
Trial*, in which capricious
powers persecute the
innocent. He died of tuberculosis; his sisters perished
in the Holocaust.

PHOTOGRAPHER UNKNOWN

ENRICO CARUSO
1873–1921

Music lessons were out of
reach for a poor Neapolitan
with 19 siblings. He made
up for lost time. At 21, with
only three years of training,
Caruso debuted in his
hometown. Soon the tenor's
prodigious voice and
dramatic delivery won
worldwide acclaim. But a
prodigious appetite for food
and tobacco shortened the
career — and life — of
opera's biggest star.

FRANK LERNER

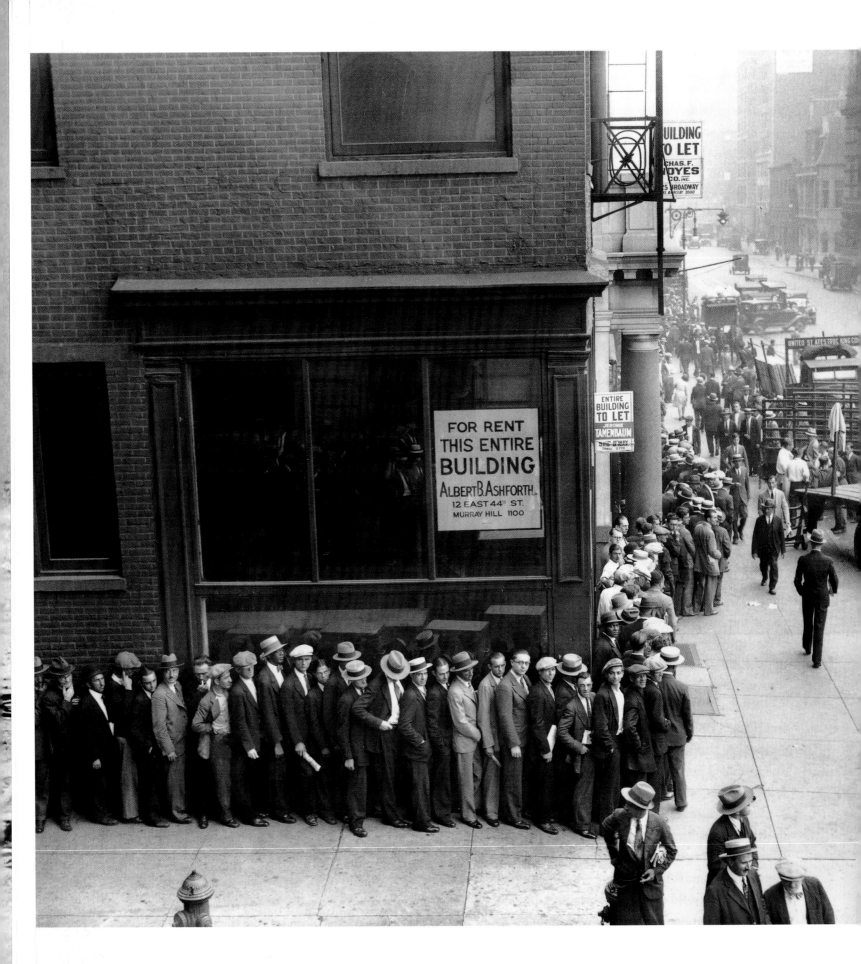

LOOK AWAY, LOOK AWAY

In 1931, Alabama cops caught 11 itinerants on a freight train. Two were white women who claimed the others, black youths aged 13 to 20, had raped them. Doctors found no evidence; yet eight of the "Scottsboro Boys" (after the town where they went on trial) were convicted and sentenced to die. The Supreme Court ruled against Alabama twice before the state gave up. Still, Clarence Norris (second from left) remained in prison until 1946.

CORBIS / BETTMANN-UPI

<

TAKE A NUMBER

On a summer day less than 10 months after the Great Crash of 1929, 6,000 New Yorkers from varying economic stations queued at a state employment agency; 135 found jobs. It would soon get worse. By 1932, almost 30 percent of America's labor force was looking for work.

CORBIS / BETTMANN-UPI

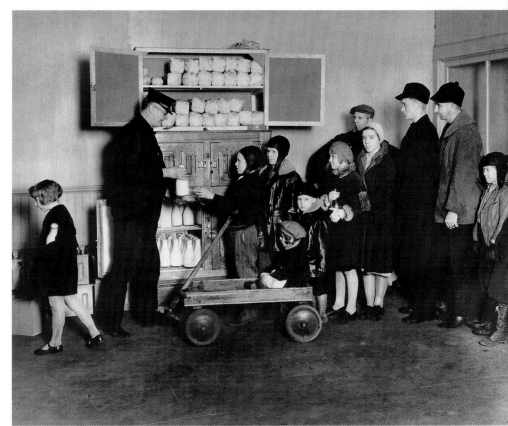

ON THE DOLE

Four days before Christmas, 1932, families in Grand Rapids, Michigan, picked up milk and bread at a fire station–cum–food bank. By this point in the Depression, industrial output had slumped 54 percent and more than 40 percent of the nation's banks had gone under or were on the verge.

AP / WIDE WORLD

POTOMAC FEVER

The capital was occupied in the summer of 1932 by some 15,000 World War I vets. In 1924, Congress had voted them a small bonus — payable in 1945. The Depression-battered men wanted their money now. A series of skirmishes with police (above) led President Herbert Hoover to call in the Army. General Douglas MacArthur's troops quickly routed the protesters and burned their tents. But the public backlash doomed Hoover's reelection bid.

RIGHT: CORBIS / BETTMANN-UNDERWOOD
INSET: NY DAILY NEWS

THE WINNING TICKET

Two-time New York governor Franklin D. Roosevelt, 50 (right, with running mate John Nance Garner, 63), was the 1932 Democratic candidate for the White House. In public, he used leg braces to hide his polio. His boilerplate speech (as in Goodland, Kansas, below) vowed "a new deal" and Prohibition's repeal. Plus, he wasn't Hoover; FDR's victory was a landslide.

RIGHT: CORBIS / BETTMANN-ACME
BELOW: AP

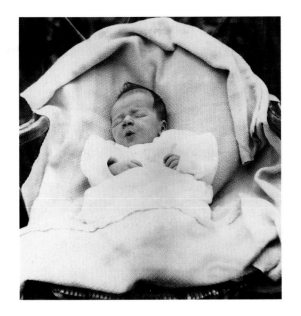

BABY TAKEN
GOOD CARE OF

LOOK FOR. INSTRU
CTIONS SATURDAY
IF POLICE GET TO
CLOSE
LOOK OUT

POST CARD
ADDRESS

CHAS. LINBERG
HOPEWELL
N.J
RUSH

THE KIDNAPPED BABY

Charles Lindbergh Jr. was 20 months old when he was taken from a second-floor bedroom of his hero father's rural New Jersey mansion on March 1, 1932. The nation was transfixed. Clues abounded (a ransom note, a ladder), as did cruel hoaxes (above right). On April 8, the Lindberghs paid $50,000 in marked bills for a fruitless tip. On May 12, their son's body was found just five miles from home. Three years passed before a German-born carpenter spent part of the $50,000. Bruno Hauptmann was electrocuted in 1936.

ABOVE: CORBIS / BETTMAN
ABOVE RIGHT: AP

AN EXPERIMENT ENDS

Jeepers, creepers! Booze was legal again! One Clevelander (lower right) couldn't wait! Prohibition was repealed in 1933 after Utah, of all states, ratified the 21st Amendment. Not until 1970 did America try more social engineering, when Congress outlawed marijuana.

NEW YORK TIMES /
ARCHIVE PHOTOS

<

A LEAGUE OF HER OWN

America's woman athlete of her time (perhaps of all time) took the gold in the javelin and the hurdles at the 1932 L.A. Olympics and lost the high jump only because the judges didn't like her unorthodox style. Babe Didrickson also starred in hoops and baseball before focusing on golf in 1934. She won 50-plus titles, including a third U.S. Women's Open at 40 despite recent cancer surgery. Babe died 26 months later, in 1956.

CORBIS / BETTMANN-UPI

> ### THE FAB FIVE

On May 28, 1934, Elzire Dionne, 24, of Callendar, Ontario, gave premature birth to her seventh, eighth, ninth, 10th and 11th babies. Émilie, Yvonne, Cécile, Marie and Annette were the first quintuplets to survive, thanks to recent advances in neonatal care. Hucksters so badly exploited the family that the tots were wards of the state until they reached seven.

KEYSTONE VIEW CO.

< ### IN NEED OF A NEW DEAL

Rural America was especially devastated by the Great Depression. In 1935, a federal relief worker (near left) visited a threadbare Tennessee family to gauge its eligibility for help. From 1933 to 1941, FDR's domestic-aid programs channeled billions to those on the brink.

CARL MYDANS / FSA

> ### DIMPLED DYNAMO

Before Shirley Temple turned eight, she was earning $2,500 per week for singing, dancing and charming in such hit movies as *Little Miss Marker* and *The Little Colonel*. Unlike many child stars before and since, Temple's life had a second act: a durable marriage and public service that included two years as U.S. ambassador to Ghana.

CULVER PICTURES

GRAPES OF WRATH

A bad drought in the Thirties teamed with bad farming practices to turn 150,000 square miles of the Great Plains into the Dust Bowl. In 1935, the well had not yet run dry on two Colorado girls (far left). But in New Mexico (above) and four other states, families called it quits and caravanned west. By decade's end, California's population had grown by 22 percent. Meanwhile, federal workers were teaching the farmers who had stayed behind better techniques for conserving topsoil.

CLOCKWISE FROM FAR LEFT: PHOTOGRAPHER UNKNOWN; DOROTHEA LANGE / FSA; LIBRARY OF CONGRESS

Beloved Badmen

A society is shaped by its laws but often defined by its outlaws. Americans bridle against authority, be it King George III or a speed-limit sign, so it is not surprising that we have long doted on a certain breed of raffish crook. The larcenous spirit of the James Gang and Billy the Kid, retailed in dime novels of the 1800s, didn't die with the Old West; it rode into the new century alongside Butch and Sundance. A rogue jaunty enough to stop while on the lam to pose for a portrait? Why, that's the stuff of folklore, not to mention Hollywood, which has lionized almost all these felons on film.

THIEVES LIKE US

In 1934, Bonnie Parker (top) was 23 and her prisoner of love, Clyde Barrow, was 25. The Dust Bowl couple indeed robbed banks, gas stations, etc. — 13 in 21 months. The law soon sprang an ambush near Gibsland, Louisiana, as deadly as the one depicted in 1968's *Bonnie and Clyde*, starring Warren Beatty and Faye Dunaway (above).

FROM TOP: CORBIS / BETTMANN-UPI; WARNER BROTHERS

DEAD AIM ON CRIME

The criminologist in J. Edgar Hoover (left) led him to modernize the FBI, which he took over in 1924, at age 29. The spin doctor in him invented the Public Enemy (usually some hood his G-men were set to nab). Hoover swore until the 1960s that there was no organized crime in America, yet kept his post through eight presidencies, until his death in 1972.

TIME INC.

WHO ARE THESE GUYS?

Robert Parker, 34 (seated, near left), went by Butch Cassidy. Harry Longbaugh, 30 (seated, far left), went by Sundance Kid. Their Wyoming-based Hole in the Wall gang of robbers and rustlers was also called The Wild Bunch (but that's another movie). Butch and Sundance did flee to Bolivia in 1901. But where did they die? Butch near Spokane in 1937, claim some, and Sundance in Casper, Wyoming, circa 1957.

HE FOUGHT THE LAW — AND THE LAW WON

As a kid in Brooklyn, Al Capone practiced crime. He perfected it in Chicago, a city thrown wide open by Prohibition. The cops couldn't nail him for the cunning massacre of rival bootleggers on St. Valentine's Day, 1929. But two years later the Feds sent him to the slammer as a tax cheat. Capone died horribly of syphilis in Miami at age 48.

AND THEN THERE WERE NONE

Having left the father of her four sons (two in prison, another dead battling Kansas cops), crime mistress Arizona "Ma" Barker, 60, met George Anderson (left). Family baby Fred objected and in 1932 killed George. In 1935, the FBI shot Fred and Ma. In 1939, son number 3, Arthur, died trying to flee Alcatraz. And in 1947, the last of Ma's boys, Lloyd, finished his 25 years in Leavenworth — only to be slain by his wife.

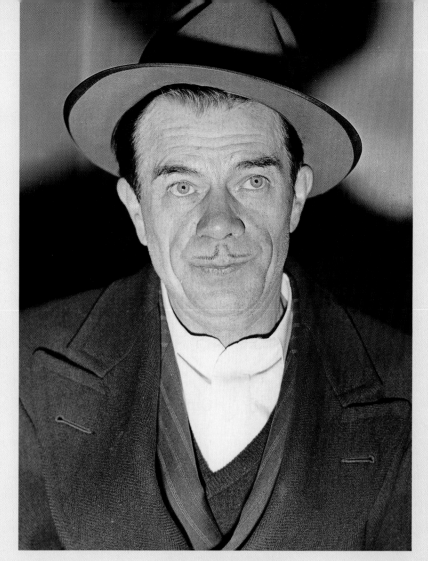

THE MONEY . . . PLEASE

He entered jail at 21 a two-bit thief and emerged at 30 far wiser. Over the next 11 months, the always polite, always dapper John Dillinger robbed at least 10 banks. Twice cops caught him; twice he escaped, hiding once at his dad's house (left) while G-men scoured the nation. In 1934, a Romanian madam in Chicago sold him out for a green card; Dillinger was 32 when he was ambushed and killed by the FBI.

AP / WIDE WORLD

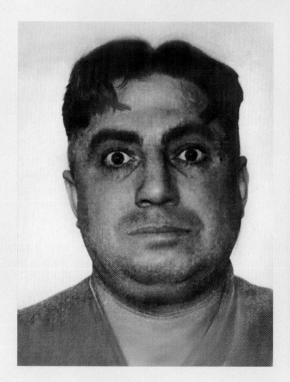

PREACHING TO THE CHOIR

In 1934, accompanied by a claque of Black Shirts, or Fascist supporters, Benito Mussolini, 51, worked a crowd in Venice. The ex-Socialist had reshaped Italy in the 12 years since becoming its youngest prime minister. Unions no longer struck, trains ran on time. Mussolini also wanted to restore Rome's imperial grandeur, so in 1935, he invaded Ethiopia.

ALFRED EISENSTAEDT / LIFE

THE GREAT ESCAPE

Mao Tse-tung, 41 (near left), and Chou En-lai, 37, had reason in 1935 to be proud. A year earlier, facing military defeat by the government, they had retreated north with 100,000 guerrillas. After 6,000 miles, 24 rivers and 18 mountain ranges, 8,000 reached safety in Yenan. In 1949, Mao's Communists won control of China; Long March veterans retained power until 1997.

LATTIMORE FOUNDATION / COURTESY OF PEABODY MUSEUM

ELIMINATING RIVALS

Many of Joseph Stalin's evil deeds in the Thirties went unreported in the USSR. Grabbing Lenin's mantle in 1926, at 47, he collectivized farms; the ensuing famine may have killed 10 million. In 1934, with Leon Trotsky banished, Stalin had his last rival, Sergey Kirov, murdered. Still ahead: the Great Purge of 1936–1938, which claimed up to 10 million more.

PHOTOGRAPHER UNKNOWN

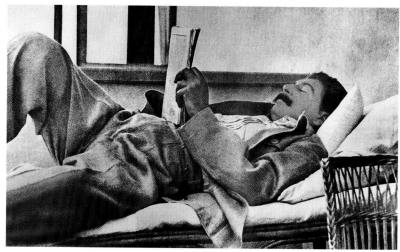

LABOR PAINS

"The chief business of the American people is business," said Calvin Coolidge in 1925. Left out of the equation: blue-collar workers, whose efforts to organize were often bloodily suppressed (Haymarket Square, Pullman, Ludlow). Management was still using goons to bust strikes (Harlan County, River Rouge) when FDR's New Deal leveled the playing field. Collective bargaining was enacted in 1935, a minimum wage in 1938. What organized labor did not — could not — anticipate was America's evolution into a service economy in which the workers' collars were white.

DOING IT THE HARD WAY

Violence was common at strikes in the Thirties. At a Pennsylvania steel mill, picketers learned firsthand that the man trying to cross their line, the Reverend H.L. Queen, was indeed a management mouthpiece (above). Less amusing was the behavior of cops at an Ohio rubber factory (left) and a machinery plant in New Jersey (below left).

ORGANIZATION MEN

When GM fired five men for wearing prolabor buttons, co-unionists in Flint, Michigan, refused to leave their plant. In launching the first large-scale peaceful sit-down strike, on December 31, 1936, they came prepared (right). After 44 days, GM gave in (below) by recognizing the United Auto Workers union.

RIGHT AND BELOW: CORBIS / BETTMANN-UNDERWOOD

WUTHERING HEIGHTS

Emily Brönte's wild moors were in Yorkshire, England. For budgetary reasons, though, Laurence Olivier, 32, and Merle Oberon, 28, had to film their roamin's in the gloamin' nearer Hollywood — even if that meant planting part of the San Fernando Valley with heather.

MOVIE STILL ARCHIVES

INTERMEZZO

Hollywood sent for Sweden's breathtaking Ingrid Bergman to re-create the role that had made her a star back home: a young pianist who falls for a married violinist. Bergman, 24, daringly left her lush eyebrows unplucked. Leslie Howard, 46, obviously didn't mind, nor did U.S. audiences.

MOVIE STILL ARCHIVES

DESTRY RIDES AGAIN

In her 12th Stateside movie, Marlene Dietrich, 38, portrayed an Old West chantoosie who wants to know what the boys in the back room will have. And what did Frenchy herself fancy? The pacifist lawman played by James Stewart.

UNIVERSAL PICTURES

THE WIZARD OF OZ

Judy Garland proved her moxie at 16 by playing a 12-year-old from Kansas. Each day her breasts had to be painfully taped flat. But she and co-stars (from left) Bert Lahr, Jack Haley and Ray Bolger ended up smiling down the Yellow Brick Road to showbiz immortality.

MOVIE STILL ARCHIVES

DARK VICTORY

She thought those vicious headaches were from dates with martini-swilling boors like Ronald Reagan, 28. In fact, they were signs of a brain tumor that would all too quickly dim Bette Davis's 31-year-old eyes.

WARNER BROTHERS

THE GREATEST YEAR IN HOLLYWOOD — EVER

THE ROARING TWENTIES

James Cagney, 40, was top-billed as a quick-fisted mobster. Humphrey Bogart, also 40, was the second banana — a not unfamiliar role. Not until 1941, in *The Maltese Falcon*, would Hollywood begin to exploit the romantic nihilism that became Bogie's trademark.

MOVIE STILL ARCHIVES

MR. SMITH GOES TO WASHINGTON

Thirty-one-year-old James Stewart's aw-shucks decency was perfect for his role as a new senator standing up to vested interests. Director Frank Capra went to Washington to show off his movie to the Capitol Hill crowd. Reviews were not kind.

COLUMBIA PICTURES

GONE WITH THE WIND

It ate up 10 writers, three directors, a cast of almost 2,500 and an inflation-adjusted budget of $48 million. Yet the 220-minute Civil War epic (intermission not included) turned out to be engrossingly intimate, thanks mostly to the star power of Vivien Leigh, 26, and Clark Gable, 38.

MGM

STAGECOACH

The vehicle was creaky — strangers joined on a perilous journey — but not John Ford's masterly direction. He reinvigorated the horse opera while making stars of John Wayne and of Arizona's scenic Monument Valley.

WALTER WANGER PRODUCTIONS

PLAYING FOR TIME

As Joseph Stalin and Nazi diplomat Joachim von Ribbentrop traded smiles in Moscow on August 23, 1939, Soviet foreign minister V.M. Molotov signed a nonaggression pact between the two archrivals that stunned the world. Nine days later (bottom left), the German army rolled into western Poland. On September 3, Ribbentrop honored a secret protocol and invited the USSR to breach Poland from the east; Stalin didn't have to be asked twice. The Soviet-German accord would last 22 months, until Hitler changed his mind.

LEFT: DEVER
BOTTOM LEFT:
HEINRICH HOFFMAN / LIFE

FUTURE SHOCK

Where was George Washington inaugurated? New York, of course, and in 1939, to mark the event's sesquicentennial, the city opened a world's fair stuffed with high-tech dreams (direct-dial long distance, TV). Over two summers, 45 million fair-goers gawked at this World of Tomorrow — while the real world was dissolving into war.

DAVID E. SCHERMAN / LIFE

Chungking, China's provisional capital, fell under savage
Japanese bombing in July 1941. Japan had begun nibbling at
China a decade earlier; it was time for the main course.

CARL MYDANS / LIFE

1940–1945

WORLD ON FIRE

VICTORY LAP IN FRANCE

Six weeks too late to enjoy April (1940) in Paris, German soldiers paraded past the Arc de Triomphe (above). In 32 days, they did what their World War I countrymen could not do in four years: occupy the French capital. To skirt the Maginot Line — a 200-mile French defense on its border with Germany — they had swept through the Low Countries, displacing thousands (like the Belgian kids, left). One 11-year-old at another refugee center: Audrey Hepburn.

ABOVE: HEINRICH HOFFMAN / LIFE
LEFT: CARL MYDANS / LIFE

ANYBODY FEEL A DRAFT?

In October 1940, the U.S. was still technically neutral, so these men at Fort Slocum, New York (right), became part of the nation's first peacetime draft. The armed forces were in sore need of bolstering: They totaled just under one million. At that time, much of Europe was Hitler's, the Battle of Britain raged on, and Germany, Japan and Italy had just formed the Axis alliance.

RALPH MORSE / LIFE

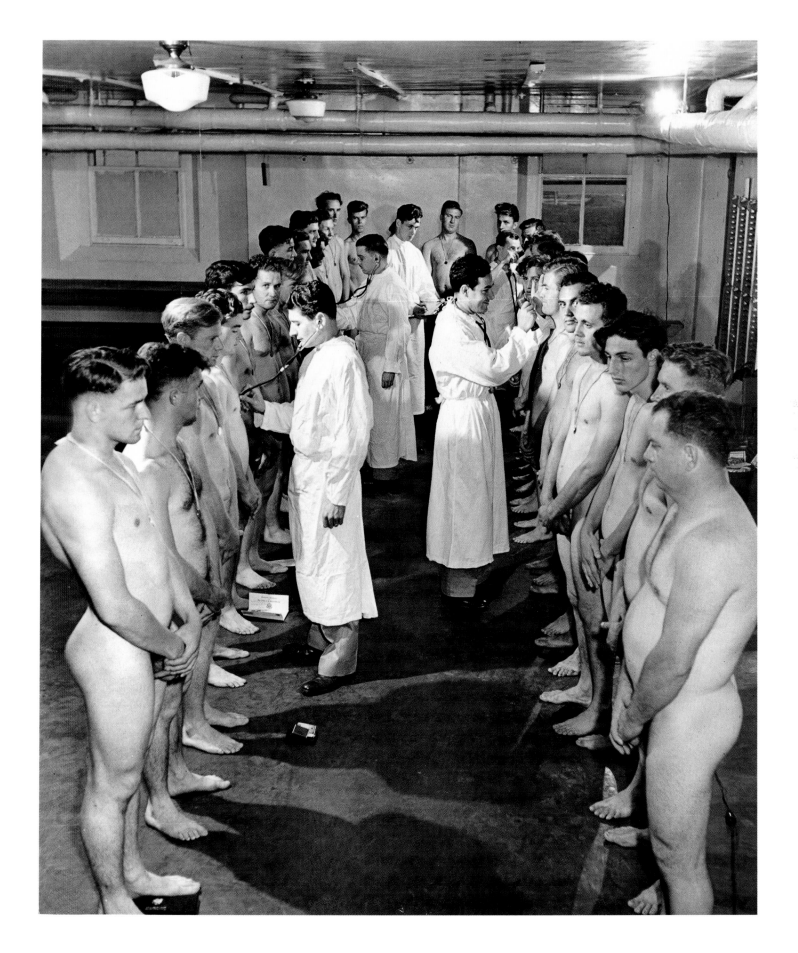

THE FIRST DESERT STORM

In January, Allied captors
herded 19,000 Italian and
6,000 German POWs to the
Libyan port of Tobruk (in the
distance, above). The west-
ward pursuit of Germany's
crack Afrika Korps ended, in
May, at Tunis (where, right,
U.S. officers surveyed their
damaged spoils of war).
North Africa was now clear
of the Axis.

ABOVE: BRITISH WAR OFFICE
RIGHT: HART PRESTON / LIFE

WHICH WAY TO ROMA?

What resistance GIs met in their July invasion of Sicily came from Germans; welcomes like that for Yanks entering Palermo (above) were routine. By then, a new government had replaced Mussolini.

ROBERT CAPA / MAGNUM

A TALE OF TWO CITIES

Soviet civilians returning to Stalingrad in February (right) found little still standing. The Wehrmacht attack, begun five months earlier, had ended in house-to-house combat. One German wrote home, "Animals flee this hell." But Hitler did win a siege in Poland (top right). In January, 65,000 Jews sealed off their Warsaw ghetto to avoid Nazi camps. They gave up in May — and were shipped to deadly Treblinka.

RIGHT: RUSSIAN NEWSREEL
ABOVE RIGHT: CORBIS /
BETTMANN

ANSWERING THE CALL

By early 1943, America's colleges were mobilizing. These students at the University of New Hampshire were obeying a War Manpower Commission directive that all students be physically fit in event of a call-up. But there would be a gender deferment; while women could enlist, the WMC promised that only "able-bodied male[s] are destined for the armed forces."

ALFRED EISENSTAEDT / LIFE

YOUNG BLUE EYES

Nights were spent at the Paramount in New York City acting as catnip to bobby-soxers and days at home in Hoboken, New Jersey, with a pair of Nancys (his first wife, 24, and their firstborn, 3). At 26, Frank Sinatra had the world on a string. The singer with the silver pipes and golden phrasing also acted and rat-packed before becoming chairman of the boored.

HERBERT GEHR / LIFE

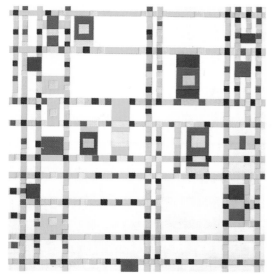

AN AUSTERE NEW ART

It looked easy: a canvas, paint, a ruler. But Dutch-born Piet Mondrian had spent two decades paring his work down to grids, an abstract minimalism soon copied by other artists and designers. In 1940, at age 68 and fearing war, he fled Europe for New York. The city's energy inspired the pulsating blocks of primary colors that infuse late Mondrians such as (above) 1943's "Broadway Boogie Woogie."

MUSEUM OF MODERN ART

HIS MAJESTY, THE DUKE

Earlier in 1943, the sidemen jamming with Edward Kennedy Ellington, 44, had accompanied him downtown to play at the Carnegie Hall premiere of *Black, Brown, & Beige*, his suite to the African-American experience. Tagged Duke in high school for his suaveness, Ellington apprenticed at Harlem's Cotton Club before becoming the century's preeminent jazz bandleader and composer.

GJON MILI / LIFE

COMBAT: 1944

Like a leaky balloon, the Axis was contracting. In North Africa, its designs were history. In the Pacific, the Allies were taking back Japan's island conquests one by one, despite a chilling new enemy tactic. In Europe, Germany was exposed both to the east, where it had been repelled by the Soviet Union, and to the south, where erstwhile partner Italy was quite unresistant to invading Americans. It was time for the Allies to go for the jugular.

THE LONGEST DAY

Though the Germans had been duped into thinking the invasion would come elsewhere, they held the high ground at Normandy. Some early Allied units dashing ashore took 90 percent casualties (above). To the rescue: air power. By nightfall, the Allies had battled up from the landing zones and taken the fight to the Germans (right). The frontal assault on Nazi-occupied Europe was on.

ABOVE: NATIONAL ARCHIVES
RIGHT: BOB LANDRY / LIFE

WRONG PLACE AND TIME

Pompeii had been hit by an act of nature; Monte Cassino was hit by U.S. bombers. The mountain southeast of Rome was crucial to the line set by Italy's German defenders against GIs fighting up the peninsula. Faulty intelligence led the Allies to target the summit monastery, built on the site where St. Benedict founded his first abbey in 529 A.D. A later raid on the base of the mountain destroyed a German-occupied town whose roots traced to pre-Roman times.

CARL MYDANS / LIFE

COMBAT: 1944

THE TICKET WAS ONE-WAY

Desperate to stem the tide, Japan in late 1944 began fitting fighter planes with 550-pound bombs; pilots were to plow them into U.S. warships (above). The gambit was called kamikaze, or divine wind, after a typhoon that repelled an invading Mongol fleet in 1274. Though the suicide flights sank or damaged some 300 ships, including the carrier *Belleau Woods* (left) most were shot down short of their target.

LEFT: EDWARD STEICHEN / U.S. NAVY
INSET: CORBIS / BETTMANN

>
EVEN IN HELL, A TIME-OUT

In one of the Pacific's grisliest theaters, a Yank found a moment to offer rations, a drink and a smile. The U.S. hit the Mariana Islands in midsummer. Worse than the brutal combat was the sight of Japanese civilians on Saipan hurling their babies, then themselves, off cliffs rather than surrender. It took Americans two months to secure Saipan, Guam and Tinian.

W. EUGENE SMITH / LIFE

HITLER BETS THE FARM

Those were brave smiles in July 1944 (inset, left). Il Duce had been rescued 10 months earlier from house arrest in Italy by a daring German commando raid. The Führer had just survived a bomb — set by his own officers — that left one arm in a sling. But even a wounded Hitler was lethal. German buzz bombs, or self-guided missiles, had begun hitting London. And in December, he mustered a massive ground strike on the Ardennes, woodlands that sprawl across France, Belgium and Luxembourg. The GI defenders (above right), denied air support by bad weather, were mauled. U.S. armor (left) proved overmatched against the enemy's new Tiger tanks. Rather than concede the Battle of the Bulge, the U.S. inserted airborne divisions (like the 82nd, right) that helped blunt the attack until skies cleared on Christmas Eve and Allied planes regained the air. America's toll: 20,000 dead, 40,000 injured, 20,000 captured. The Germans fared worse. Hitler was now staring at Götterdämmerung.

LEFT: GEORGE SILK / LIFE
INSET: HEINRICH HOFFMAN / LIFE
RIGHT: U.S. ARMY (2)

> STRETCHING TO NEW HEIGHTS

Freed perhaps by the stirring strings that open *Appalachian Spring*, Aaron Copland's 1944 celebration of pastoral America, Martha Graham, 50, high-kicked loose of the jagged gestures she had championed for two decades. Drawn at 22 to modern dance, Graham's daring choreography and musical tastes prodded her art beyond its classical ballet origins.

JERRY COOKE / LIFE

NAME THAT TUNE

In 1944, Paul Robeson, 46, took the mike to sing: a) spirituals; b) "Ol' Man River"; c) the national anthem of an Allied nation. Answer: c ("Hymn of the Soviet Union"). A Rutgers football All-America who spurned the baby NFL to flex his magnificent bass onstage, Robeson in the mid-1930s grew sick of racism and embraced Communism. In 1950, the U.S. lifted his passport (and ruined his career). The singer-actor lived until 1976.

HERBERT GEHR / LIFE

AN EDDY OF ECONOMISTS

War still boiled on three continents, but envoys of 44 nations met during the summer of 1944 in quiet Bretton Woods, New Hampshire, to plan the rebuilding to come. Led by free-marketers John Maynard Keynes of Britain (near left) and U.S. Treasury boss Henry Morgenthau (taking notes), they devised a series of instruments — including the World Bank — to speed postwar recovery. For once, the science of economics wasn't dismal.

ALFRED EISENSTAEDT / LIFE

THE GAME MUST GO ON

In 1945, though minus an arm since a boyhood mishap, Pete Gray, 30, made the bigs. World War II had drained the rosters of the 16 major league teams. Thus Joe Nuxhall hurled for the Cincinnati Reds at age 15 and outfielder Gray hit .218 in 77 games for the St. Louis Browns (a sad-sack team that six years later sent Eddie Gaedel, a 43-inch-tall midget, to the plate to coax a walk).

AP

Prelude to Slaughter

In early 1945, five Marines and a Navy medic were fixed in time raising the Stars and Stripes on Iwo Jima — and the morale of war-weary Americans at home. Minutes after capturing probably the most memorable image of the Pacific conflict (above), AP photojournalist Joe Rosenthal, 33, recorded another (right) that is less famous but more haunting. The leathernecks were cheering because it had taken their unit just four days to conquer 500-foot Mount Suribachi, the highest point on this desolate, eight-square-mile volcanic atoll in the West Pacific. Forgotten in the joyous moment: the cruel lessons of island combat. Because Iwo sat within easy flying range of Japan's Home Islands, it was defended by 23,000 troops. The Imperial troops fought on for another month, until only 216 were alive to surrender. Of the 30,000-plus Americans who waded ashore, 21,000 were wounded and 6,800 killed. Among the dead: three of Rosenthal's flag raisers.

JOE ROSENTHAL / AP (2)

HELL IN THE PACIFIC

Okinawa was not a minor Pacific atoll but one of Japan's southernmost Home Islands. Its fortifications were exceptional (right). Joining the April invasion was journalist Ernie Pyle, 44 (inset), already a Pulitzer winner for his reporting from North Africa and Europe. He was killed by enemy fire on April 9. Fighting on Okinawa continued until August.

RIGHT: W. EUGENE SMITH / LIFE
INSET: U.S. SIGNAL CORPS

<

HE KEPT HIS WORD

In January 1945, almost three years after Douglas MacArthur, his wife and their son had been ordered to evacuate the Philippines ahead of the approaching Japanese, the general, 64, strolled back through the surf at Lingayen Gulf. He was fulfilling his pledge, "I shall return." MacArthur brought 68,000 U.S. troops. In July, he pronounced the islands liberated.

CARL MYDANS / LIFE

<

THE NEXT WAR BEGINS

February 1945: To Yalta, a Crimean resort, traveled Winston Churchill, 70 (far left); Franklin D. Roosevelt, 63; and host Joseph Stalin, 65. With no other Allied leaders present, they devised a strategy to checkmate the Axis and drew up a postwar map. Stalin came away with rights to Eastern Europe. The seeds of the Cold War were sown.

NATIONAL ARCHIVES /
U.S. ARMY

A CHIEF'S LAST HAIL

On April 12, 1945, polio patients at the Warm Springs spa (below), in Georgia, honored fellow victim Franklin D. Roosevelt, dead at 63 while there for therapy. Then, accordionist Graham Jackson, USN (left), began playing through his tears. FDR was the only four-time president; terms were capped at two in 1951. His successor: Harry S Truman.

EDWARD CLARK / LIFE (2)

HALFWAY TO PEACE

From New York — where a replica Lady Liberty greeted the masses gathering in Times Square — to Los Angeles, America partied on May 7, 1945, as word spread of Germany's surrender. It came 68 months and 50 million deaths after Hitler invaded Poland. But VE (Victory in Europe) Day jubilation was tempered; there was a war yet to be won in the Pacific.

TONY LINCK / LIFE

AUGUST 6, 1945

The silvery speck in the morning sky over
Hiroshima, Japan, raised no alarms. What
havoc could a lone U.S. B-29 wreak? From
Enola Gay's belly fell a single 9,000-pound
bomb that detonated 2,000 feet above ground
zero. The force of its fission-generated,
5,400-degree fireball killed 80,000 and leveled
a four-mile-wide circle. The radioactivity
spread by the mushroom cloud would claim
an estimated 120,000 more lives by 1950.

BERNARD HOFFMAN / LIFE

Pandora's Box

Though Shakespeare wrote of "atomies," not until the 1930s did anyone suspect that one of nature's tiniest building blocks harbored energy of undreamt scope. And then the atomic weapon — plausibly imagined in 1936's *The Dark Frontier* by Eric Ambler, father of the modern thriller — was soon a reality. War has a way of both hastening and mutating technology; Alfred Nobel cooked up dynamite to help farmers clear tree stumps. The fallout from the only two A-bombs dropped in anger will not dissipate. One casualty: nuclear energy, an industry undone by a string of accidental meltdowns. Another: our psyches. Forget disarmament. We know those early bombs are puny next to what now fits in a terrorist's valise. But like the genie, knowledge cannot be returned.

> ELEMENTARY DEDUCTIONS

For explaining a phenomenon first observed in 1898 — that the metallic element uranium radiates mysterious particles — Marie and Pierre Curie (top right) became, in 1903, the first husband-and-wife Nobel winners. The Polish-born Mme. Curie, 36, coined the word *radioactivity*. But handling radioactive samples led to pernicious anemia, from which she died in 1934. By then, a team at Cambridge University in England, led by Ernest Rutherford (center, with cigarette) had for the first time split an atom (of nitrogen). And later that decade, America's Ernest Lawrence (bottom right) had progressed from a crude 1930 prototype to an advanced model of his cyclotron, a particle accelerator essential to the new science called nuclear physics.

FROM TOP: TIME INC.;
CAMBRIDGE UNIVERSITY PRESS;
GRANGER COLLECTION

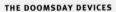

< THE DOOMSDAY DEVICES

Replicas of the first two A-bombs sit in a science museum in Los Alamos, New Mexico. Little Boy (far left) was dropped on Hiroshima, Fat Man on Nagasaki four days later, killing 40,000. Why was Germany not also targeted? It had surrendered before the first successful test blast on July 16, 1945.

BEN MARTIN / TIME

WHAT HIS MIND FORESAW

When Albert Einstein, 59, posed for this sketch in 1938, scientists in the U.S., England, France and Germany were racing to unlock the secrets of the atom. The next January, a German team came upon a process, fission, that could in theory transform uranium into a superbomb. When Einstein — a Jewish Nobel Laureate who upon Hitler's rise in 1933 had fled to the U.S. — learned of the news, he used his stature to alert the White House. In mid-1940, FDR responded by setting up the hush-hush Manhattan Project. Einstein, ironically, was not asked to join. The physicist, whose $E = mc^2$ fundamentally changed the way man understood his universe, was a known pacifist and Zionist, and thus deemed politically unreliable.

ELIOT ELISOFON

On the blackboard:

$$mob = \frac{h}{2\pi}l$$

$$r_0 = \frac{e^2}{m}$$

MANHATTAN TRANSFER

Who better in America to test the fission theory than Italian émigré Enrico Fermi (left), who had just won the 1938 Nobel for physics? He built a reactor beneath the decrepit University of Chicago football stadium (top left — the school had quit the Big Ten). On December 2, 1942, Fermi, 41, and his team achieved a sustained chain reaction. The superbomb was no longer just theory.

TOP LEFT: ARGONNE NATIONAL LABORATORY
LEFT: NEW YORK HERALD TRIBUNE

UNDER WESTERN SKIES

Even as Fermi was validating fission, physicist J. Robert Oppenheimer, 38 (above), and Army general Leslie Groves, who had just finished overseeing construction of the Pentagon, were turning 77 square miles of New Mexico mesa into a top-secret research complex. The army of scientists who came to work at Alamagordo needed almost 26 months to build the first A-bomb. Test date: July 16, 1945, over Trinity, New Mexico.

FRITZ GORO / LIFE

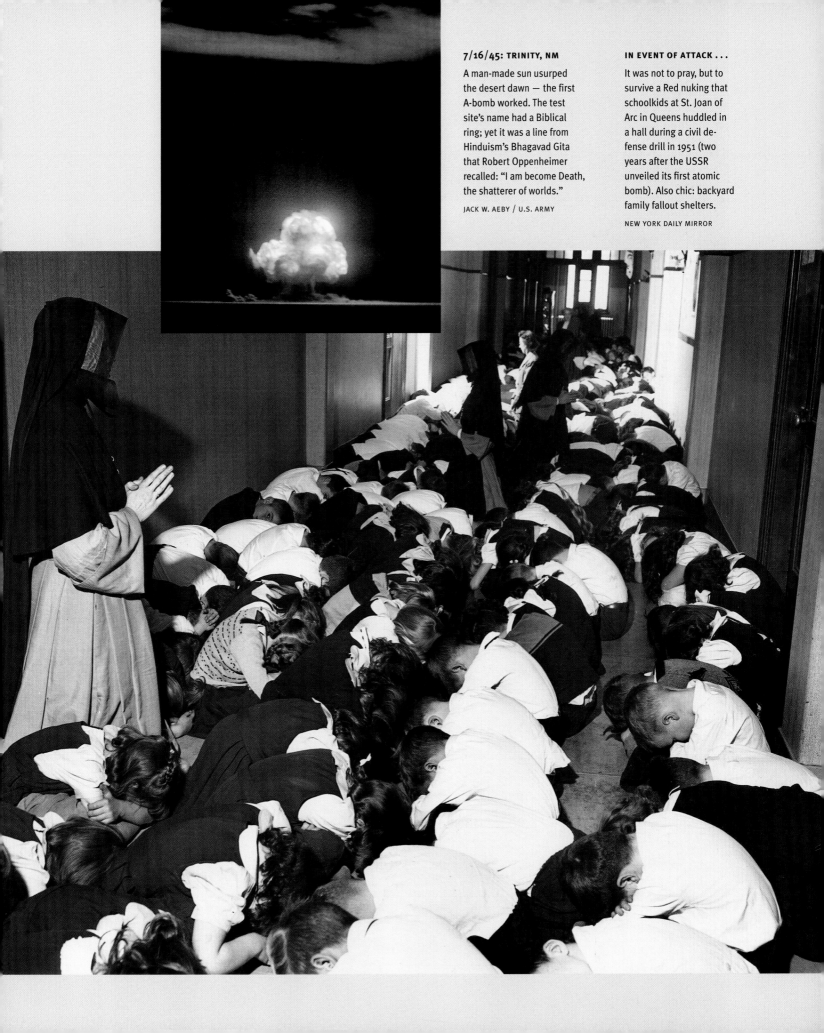

7/16/45: TRINITY, NM

A man-made sun usurped the desert dawn — the first A-bomb worked. The test site's name had a Biblical ring; yet it was a line from Hinduism's Bhagavad Gita that Robert Oppenheimer recalled: "I am become Death, the shatterer of worlds."

JACK W. AEBY / U.S. ARMY

IN EVENT OF ATTACK . . .

It was not to pray, but to survive a Red nuking that schoolkids at St. Joan of Arc in Queens huddled in a hall during a civil defense drill in 1951 (two years after the USSR unveiled its first atomic bomb). Also chic: backyard family fallout shelters.

NEW YORK DAILY MIRROR

MORE BANG FOR THE BUCK

A thermonuclear palette vivified the night skies of Hawaii on July 9, 1962. Some 800 miles to the west, the Pentagon had just detonated another H-bomb 200 miles over Johnston Island. The first hydrogen bomb — 500 times more powerful than the A-bomb — had been triggered by the U.S. in 1952. By the time the heavens over Honolulu turned green, Moscow already had a working copy.

J.R. EYERMAN / LIFE

DEADLY CARGO

That white stalk being transferred aboard a U.S. nuclear sub at Holy Loch, Scotland, in 1969 was a Polaris intercontinental ballistic missile with a 600-kiloton payload and a 1,200-mile range. At the height of the arms race, the U.S. and the USSR had more than 75,000 nukes aimed at each other.

BILL RAY / LIFE

THE CHERNOBYL SYNDROME

Until April 28, 1986, it was a thriller movie plot, not a real concern among nuclear physicists: a runaway reactor that bores straight through the earth to China. Yes, there was that radioactive leak at Three Mile Island, Pennsylvania, but it was minor. Then came the meltdown at Chernobyl (right), a shoddily built, poorly run Soviet plant in Ukraine. Immediate dead: 31. Long-term dead: 125,000 — and counting.

SHONE / GAMMA LIAISON

TIME TO STAND DOWN

A Soviet sentry guarded ICBMs (below) slated to be scrapped under a 1987 disarmament treaty between the U.S. and USSR. Not affected: the 10 other nations known or thought to have such arsenals. The threat of thermonuclear warfare has eased — but it is far from ended.

AFP

REQUIEM

GEORGE WASHINGTON CARVER, 1861–1943

Born a slave in Missouri, he set out at 12 in quest of an education. Two decades later, the agricultural chemist was at Tuskegee Institute, devising new uses for then-unpopular crops like peanuts. By promoting crop diversification, Carver altered farming worldwide.

CORBIS / BETTMANN-ACME

BEATRIX POTTER 1866–1943

Love of animals, starting with her own pooch, suffuses the British writer-illustrator's charming (yet never cloying) tales. Peter Rabbit debuted in a letter, graced with her own drawings, sent by the 27-year-old Potter to an ailing child. Later would come Squirrel Nutkin, Benjamin Bunny and Jemima Puddle-Duck.

ARCHIVE PHOTOS

GLENN MILLER
1904–1944

Benny Goodman may have had more swing, but this bandleader's sweet renditions of "In the Mood" and "Tuxedo Junction" put his ensemble atop the charts in the early 1940s. Its signature piece was the Miller composition "Moonlight Serenade." He was touring with an Air Force orchestra when his plane from London to Paris disappeared over the English Channel.

CORBIS / BETTMANN-UPI

FERDINAND MORTON
1890–1941

Answering to "Jelly Roll" and flashing a diamond-studded front tooth, he liked to boast that jazz was his personal invention. The pianist, who had refined his chops by pounding ivory in the bordellos of New Orleans, wasn't totally off-key. By sketching out scores that allowed musicians room to riff, Morton helped push ragtime and Dixieland toward jazz.

CHARLES PETERSEN

<
VIRGINIA WOOLF
1882–1941

To the salon she established with her siblings in London's Bloomsbury district went England's leading intellectuals. That hothouse atmosphere led to the essays and fiction that won her fame as a belletrist. Her pointed wit, affirmed in journals and letters published after her suicide, showed why many were afraid of Virginia Woolf.

MAN RAY

EDVARD MUNCH
1863–1944

The raw emotionalism of his most famous (and most parodied) painting, "The Scream," is also evident in this 1939 self-portrait. The Norwegian artist had reason to express an angst-tortured view of the world on canvas and in woodcuts. Munch lost his mother, as well as his sister, to tuberculosis before he reached adulthood.

ERICH LESSING / ART RESOURCE

F. SCOTT FITZGERALD
1896–1940

Through novels about care-
less strivers, the Minne-
sotan earned the social and
material success he craved.
Fitzgerald and his writer
wife, Zelda (above), were
happy to be role models for
flapperdom. But his master-
piece, *The Great Gatsby*,
foreshadowed the collapse
of both the Jazz Age and the
couple. She was institutionalized for schizophrenia; he
drifted into alcoholism.
TIME INC.

<
LOU GEHRIG
1903–1941

Lured by the New York
Yankees from Columbia
University, the slugging first
baseman (493 career
homers) set an endurance
mark thought untouchable:
2,130 straight games. It was
broken in 1995 (by Cal
Ripken Jr.), leaving only a
sad medical legacy:
Amyotrophic lateral scle-
rosis, which ended his life,
is usually referred to as
Lou Gehrig's disease.
AP / WIDE WORLD

<
CAROLE LOMBARD
1908–1942

She went from junior high directly to silent-era Hollywood. There, Lombard enhanced her glamour with a sense of timing learned from slapstick master Mack Sennett and achieved stardom in screwball comedies like 1934's *Twentieth Century*. A happy second marriage, to Clark Gable, ended when her plane to a war-bond rally crashed near Las Vegas.

CORBIS / BETTMANN-INP

EMMA GOLDMAN
1869–1940

For urging Yanks to resist the draft in World War I, the Russian-Jewish anarchist was deported home in 1919. Red Emma soured on the Bolsheviks and became one of the first leftists to condemn the Soviets. Moving to Western Europe, she was soon railing against Hitler.

CHICAGO HISTORICAL SOCIETY

AIMEE SEMPLE MCPHERSON
1890–1944

The cross wasn't all that the flamboyant evangelist embraced. Three years after opening a $1.5 million temple in L.A., she vanished. Sister Aimee reappeared five weeks later claiming kidnappers had held her in a shack on the Mexican border. In fact, she had been shacked up with a married man. The faithful couldn't care less.

CORBIS / BETTMANN-INP

1946–1963

SPREADING THE WEALTH

In war, it had been guns or butter.
In postwar America, the choice
came down to baseball or piano.
(This 1962 recital was by Jimmy
Childs, 9, of Manchester, Iowa.)

YALE JOEL / LIFE

Crimes and Punishments

History being writ by the victors, in 1945 the Allies put on trial 24 Nazis (including Hermann Göring, left) and 27 Japanese leaders (including Hideki Tojo, in the dock, above). Beyond reach were Hitler, dead by his own hand, and Mussolini, shot sneaking back to Milan where his corpse was hung in public; Hirohito escaped judgment by using his vested majesty to ensure a peaceful U.S. occupation of his nation. At Nuremberg, Reichsmarschall Göring, 53, was condemned to death; on the eve of his hanging, he gagged down a smuggled cyanide capsule. At Tokyo, Prime Minister Tojo, 64 — who the previous September had shot himself in the chest but survived — received the same sentence; he climbed the gallows in 1948.

LEFT: RALPH MORSE / LIFE; ABOVE: CARL MYDANS / LIFE

A YOUNG DIARIST-TO-BE

A slim volume that appeared in Dutch bookstores in 1947 was by the girl who is second to right in this snapshot taken 10 years before. But in 1942, she and her family, which was Jewish, had to hide in Nazi-occupied Amsterdam. They were betrayed in 1944; she died, at 15, in Bergen-Belsen. The slim volume was Anne Frank's heartbreaking diary of those two years in hiding. (Three of her playmates survived the Holocaust.)

ILSE LEDERMAN

<

TO COIN A PHRASE

To Fulton, Missouri, on March 5, 1947, came President Harry Truman, 62, and bestogied private citizen Winston Churchill, 72. The man who willed Britain through the war had stunningly been voted from office 11 weeks after VE Day. But he had not lost his grasp of geopolitics. In a speech that day, Churchill warned, "An iron curtain has descended across the Continent."

GEORGE SKADDING / LIFE

A NATION'S THANKS

Charles Smayda wasn't like most fellow students at the University of Iowa in 1947. He was older, he had a family — and his bills were paid by Uncle Sam. The GI Bill of 1944 promised servicemen financial help. In just its first 20 years, the act, extended to cover Korea vets, enabled 10 million to go to school and 6.2 million to buy homes.

MARGARET BOURKE-WHITE / LIFE

MARSHALL'S PLAN

As a five-star general, he helped plot the Allied victory. In 1947, as Secretary of State, George C. Marshall, 67, toured Europe (right), then proposed a reconstruction plan that could run $20 billion over four years. Congress didn't blink and said yes.

THOMAS D. MCAVOY / LIFE

OPERATION RESCUE

Overflying a part of Berlin still in ruins in 1948, a USAF C-54 arrived laden with cargo. In June, the USSR had cut all land and river links to the city, which lay 110 miles inside East Germany. To supply 2.5 million Berliners with life's necessities, America and Britain began an airlift that averaged 625 flights daily for 318 days.

CHARLES F. JACOBS / BLACK STAR

VOYAGE OF THE DAMNED

The postwar destination of many vessels packed with displaced Jews (like the ragtag *Szold*, right), was Palestine — Biblical Israel. All were turned away by the British, overseers of the territory since 1922. The cruel 1947 rejection of the ship *Exodus*, recounted in a book and a film, turned international public opinion against London. On May 14, 1948, the modern state of Israel was founded as a homeland for world Jewry.

DAVID DOUGLAS DUNCAN

ONE IS A LONELY NUMBER

Jackie Robinson (above, stealing home in 1948) was the object of much attention — and vilification. The UCLA graduate had been chosen to break the national pastime's color barrier by Branch Rickey, 66, general manager of the Brooklyn Dodgers (right, with grandson). Pro football had already accepted black fullback Marion Motley of the Cleveland Browns, and the baseball sage knew that a number of Negro league players, among them, Robinson, could help his team. He was right. By 1953, six of the 16 big league teams were suiting up blacks. Last to integrate: the Boston Red Sox, who called up Pumpsie Green in 1959.

ABOVE: HY PESKIN / LIFE
RIGHT: GEORGE SILK / LIFE

CALL HIM SKY KING

That sharp clap of a sonic boom over California on October 14, 1947, came from this jet piloted by this cockpit stud, Chuck Yeager, 24. The plane (named for his wife) was the first craft to fly faster than the speed of sound under its own power. Some had feared the X-1 might disintegrate. When it passed 700 mph and didn't, gone was the barrier to the jet age in military and commercial flight.

CORBIS / BETTMANN-UPI

THE BABE GOES IVY

Three months before his death from cancer, good-field, great-hit Yankee outfielder Babe Ruth, 53, donated his papers to Yale University. Accepting them in New Haven, Connecticut, on June 5, 1948, was the captain of the Eli team. Perhaps the first baseman, 23, knew his own scouting report (good field, no hit); George Bush chose a game other than baseball.

YALE UNIVERSITY

WELCOME TO THE BURBS

The new instant community outside Los Angeles at right was one of a rash put up by developers in the immediate postwar years. In Long Island's Levittown, two bedrooms and a slice of lawn could be had for $6,990. Growing up in such tract houses would not affect speech patterns until, like, wow, the 1980s?

LOOMIS DEAN / LIFE

A PASSAGE FROM INDIA

By ending its 89-year colonial rule of India in 1947, Britain washed its hands of the violent, age-old rivalry between Hindus and Muslims. (Below, casualties in Calcutta were a grisly feast for vultures.) Partitioning off the new state of Pakistan for minority Muslims set off more violence. Most prominent of the million-plus victims: Mohandas Gandhi (inset), assassinated in 1948 by a fellow Hindu for his pacifist, nonpartisan views.

MARGARET BOURKE-WHITE / LIFE (2)

>
CRY THE BELOVED COUNTRY

Historically, South Africa's 11 million nonwhites shared few of the rights enjoyed by the nation's 2.5 million whites. In 1948, after parliament was won by ultrasegregationists, they had even fewer. The harsh new law of the land, called apartheid, regulated every facet of nonwhite life, from public facilities (like an oceanside bench in Durban, right) to marriage (not with a white).

N.R. FARBMAN / LIFE

ACQUIRING A NEW HABIT

The 99.9 percent of Americans who owned no TVs in 1948 began changing their minds when two prime-time pioneers became must-watch phenomenons. Comic Milton Berle, 40 (far right, with Judy Canova), locked up Tuesday night so tightly that movie houses and bars suffered; NBC soon re-upped him for 30 years at $200,000 per. Sunday night belonged to a CBS variety hour hosted by gossip columnist Ed Sullivan, 45 (at mike, right). Among his opening night guests: Jerry Lewis, 22, with arms crossed; past him, Richard Rodgers and Oscar Hammerstein; and past the host's left shoulder, Dean Martin, 31. Budget for this "really big shew": $1,375.

RIGHT: CBS PHOTO ARCHIVE
FAR RIGHT: RALPH MORSE / LIFE

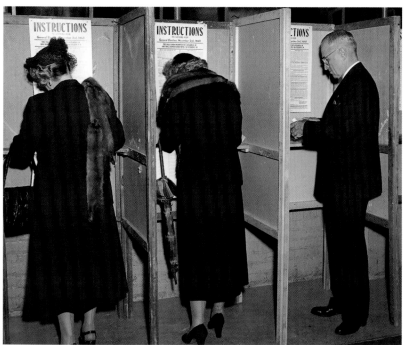

EVERY VOTE COUNTS

Election Day, 1948: Casting ballots in Independence, Missouri (pop. 30,000 plus), were, from left, Margaret Truman, 24; her mother, Bess, 63; and her father, Harry, 64. If Dad looked subdued, it was because all opinion polls projected a comfortable win for presidential challenger Thomas E. Dewey. Wrong.

AP

>

TWO-PIECE BOMBSHELL

Itsy-bitsy teeny-weeny, the Louis Reard creation wasn't. Still, a stunned Paris fashion press was quick to dub it "bikini," after the atoll in the Pacific where the U.S. tested nukes. Starchy French resorts insisted on one-piece suits. Along the Riviera, they complied by tanking the tops.

NINA LEEN / LIFE

>
WHO NEEDS A BRUSH?

A half century after being mocked as Jack the Dripper, Wyoming-born Jackson Pollock won U.S. Postal Service endorsement. The artist began to drizzle paint on canvas in the late 1940s; those early works helped launch the abstract expressionist school. (The Postal Service took artistic license in basing its stamp on a Martha Holmes photo; it painted out Pollock's ever-present cigarette.)

U.S. POSTAL SERVICE

NEW LAND WAR IN ASIA

The refugees streaming into Yongdungpo, near Seoul (left), in 1951 bespoke the war racking their country. Korea had been freed from a long Japanese occupation in 1945 — only to be split at the 38th parallel in 1948. The North (capital: P'yŏng-yang) fell under Soviet rule, while the South (capital: Seoul) became a republic. On June 25, 1950, the North mounted a massive inva-sion. Two weeks later, the U.N.'s first multinational police force — at that time, 18,000 troops provided by the U.S. — began landing at Pusan. Douglas MacArthur, 70, was recalled to duty to head the force, which won back lost territory and drove into the North. But in November, Communist China entered the fray; soon, U.S. troops were retreating south down the mountainous peninsula (top right). Combat see-sawed into 1951 (middle right, GIs under fire near Anyang), with American air power (bottom right, a snow-covered carrier) par-tially checked by the new Soviet MiG-15 fighter jet. In April, when MacArthur vowed to cross the Yalu River to fight Chinese troops in China, Truman fired him. Truce talks, begun in late 1951, were finally concluded in mid-1953. But at century's end, there was still no peace.

CLOCKWISE FROM LEFT:
CARL MYDANS / LIFE;
DAVID DOUGLAS DUNCAN;
JOHN DOMINIS / LIFE (2)

DID SOMEONE SAY SUSHI?

In 1951, to coax Lucille Ball to TV, CBS met two demands. Real-life hubby Desi Arnaz, Cuban accent and all, would be in the sitcom (with Vivian Vance, left, and William Frawley). And though most other network shows originated live from New York, with only a few saved on low-res kinescopes, Ball, 40, would stay in L.A. and do her shows on film. This meant *I Love Lucy*'s slapstick could be sharpened by editing — and its episodes could be rerun for all time.

SEMI-FAST FOOD

When U.S. stores began to stock a new frozen-food product in 1954, television had penetrated into 26 million households, up from 172,000 in 1948. TV dinners took only 25 minutes to cook. Though they tasted like K rations, many a World War II and Korea vet scarfed them up without a beef.

1946–1963: SPREADING THE WEALTH

They Had a Dream

The first ship bearing Africans to America most likely docked at Jamestown, Virginia, in 1619. From the start, slavery divided the country's whites, who eventually settled their differences with arms. The Civil War freed the nation's blacks. But left intact were the legacies of bondage, the cruelest of which was the perception that skin color mattered. Epic legislation, earned with tears, sweat and blood, has spelled out basic civil rights but not put an end to racism. Which is ironic. If the geneticists have it right, everyone living in the United States is an African-American, descended — like the rest of humanity — from the people who ranged the sub-Saharan tropics 400,000 years ago.

SUFFER THE CHILDREN

It was not the classroom her parents wanted for Linda Brown, 10 (wearing scarf). But a school 17 blocks nearer their Topeka, Kansas, home was whites only. The Browns sued the school board in 1952. On May 17, 1954, the nine white justices of the U.S. Supreme Court ruled that in "public education, the doctrine of separate but equal has no place." The decision would affect 11 million white and black students in 17 states.

CARL IWASAKI / LIFE

TURNING NEITHER CHEEK

W.E.B. Du Bois's 1903 book, *The Souls of Black Folk*, rejected the tolerance of racism favored by Booker T. Washington. In 1910, at 42, the sociologist (Harvard's first black Ph.D.) co-founded the NAACP. Du Bois grew impatient with the movement's slow progess and, late in life, renounced his U.S. citizenship. He died in Ghana one year before the Civil Rights Act of 1964.

CULVER PICTURES

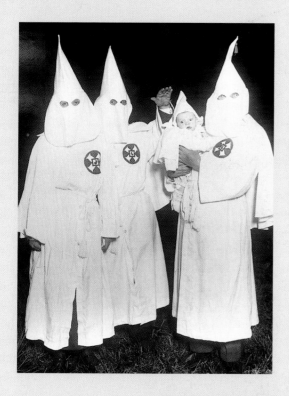

JIM CROW IN KHAKI

Finished with basic training at Fort Huachuca, Arizona, in August 1943, the all-black 93rd Infantry Division was set to go. By then, the all-black Tuskegee Airmen were already dogfighting with distinction in Europe. Still, though more than one million African-Americans served in World War II, most were relegated to labor battalions. And those who did see action fought in segregated units.

CHARLES STEINHEIMER / LIFE

MOVE? NOT THIS TIME

She paid the bus fare, so despite local law (blacks to the back), seamstress Rosa Parks, then 42, decided not to give up her seat to a white man. When she was hauled into court four days later, on December 5, 1955, blacks in Montgomery, Alabama, stopped taking buses. The boycott, led by the Reverend Martin Luther King Jr., 26, ran for 381 days, until the Supreme Court struck down the ordinance.

PAUL SCHUTZER / LIFE

>
THE CROSSING GUARDS

Even the mayor didn't want this to happen: the 101st Airborne in front of Central High in September 1957, ready to take on not only white supremacists but also the Arkansas National Guard. Why? So nine black students could enroll. Governor Orval Faubus, 47, had resisted integration by calling out his Guard. Seeing schoolkids rebuffed at bayonet-point, Ike sent in paratroopers.

JOHN BRYSON

BEAUTIFUL DREAMER

On August 28, 1963, before some 250,000 fellow citizens thronging the Mall in Washington, D.C., and uncounted millions watching on live TV, Martin Luther King Jr., 34, related his vision for a more equitable America. King had flaws. (The FBI gathered personal dirt in an effort to shut him up.) But his strengths — passion, soaring language — pushed the civil rights movement over the top.

FRANCIS MILLER / LIFE

<

ETHICAL FOOD FIGHT

Unreconstructed Southerners (like these in March 1960 in Nashville) did not take kindly to the new civil rights strategy of passive resistance. Blacks would not leave whites-only lunch counters until served. Chains like Woolworth's (at whose Greensboro, North Carolina, store the first sit-in occurred) were too timid to do the right thing.

VIC COOLEY / NASHVILLE BANNER

MISSING CALL FBI

THE FBI IS SEEKING INFORMATION CONCERNING THE DISAPPEARANCE AT PHILADELPHIA, MISSISSIPPI, OF THESE THREE INDIVIDUALS ON JUNE 21, 1964. EXTENSIVE INVESTIGATION IS BEING CONDUCTED TO LOCATE GOODMAN, CHANEY, AND SCHWERNER, WHO ARE DESCRIBED AS FOLLOWS:

ANDREW GOODMAN	JAMES EARL CHANEY	MICHAEL HENRY SCHWERNER

RACE:	White	Negro	White
SEX:	Male	Male	Male
DOB:	November 23, 1943	May 30, 1943	November 6, 1939
POB:	New York City	Meridian, Mississippi	New York City
AGE:	20 years	21 years	24 years
HEIGHT:	5'10"	5'7"	5'9" to 5'10"
WEIGHT:	150 pounds		

MARTYRS TO THE CAUSE

The three, who were devoting the summer of 1964 to registering rural black Mississippians to vote, were last seen on a dirt road in Neshoba County. They had been stopped for speeding. Six weeks later, their tortured and bullet-riddled corpses were dug up near the town of Philadelphia. Seven locals were convicted, including the chief deputy sheriff of Neshoba County.

CORBIS / BETTMANN-UPI

MARCH ON SELMA

Word obviously had not reached law enforcers in Selma, Alabama, that nine months earlier President Lyndon B. Johnson had signed the Civil Rights Act of 1964. The cops soon busted blacks trying to sign up to vote. Those arrests sparked several mass marches. (After one, the KKK shot dead civil rights worker Viola Liuzzo, 38.) That summer, Congress passed the Voting Rights Act of 1965.

FRANK DANDRIDGE / LIFE

A U.S. BENCHMARK

On October 2, 1967, with a hand from wife Cecilia, Thurgood Marshall, 59, prepared to be sworn in as the Supreme Court's 96th — and first black — justice. His legal views were no mystery to LBJ, who named him, nor to the Senate, which confirmed him (by 69–11). Just 14 years earlier, Marshall had stood before the Court to argue the landmark *Brown* v. *Board of Ed*.

AP / WIDE WORLD

<

A SWEET VICTORY

Had this store in Peachtree, Alabama, ever drawn such a queue? But on May 3, 1966, they were there to vote, not to buy. Racial discrimination was now a federal crime, as were voter-competency tests and poll taxes. So for the first time, blacks of Wilcox County, who outnumbered whites by nearly three-to-one, had a say in how they were governed.

CORBIS / BETTMANN-UPI

ON THE ROAD AGAIN

He was easy to parody: the ear-catching speeches, briskly rhymed; the eye-catching photo ops, nicely timed. But the Reverend Jesse Jackson (above, 42, during his 1984 White House run) had an agenda beyond glory. His voter-turnout drives and candidacies were a message to blacks that the ballot was theirs to use — or lose.

BRUCE TALAMON

TIME TO SMELL THE ROSES

Colin Powell, first black to head the Joint Chiefs, had overseen Desert Storm, so now, in 1993, with wife Alma, he gave the last salute of a 35-year career. The Army was still segregated as he grew up in New York during World War II. His time was Vietnam (10.5 percent of U.S. troops were black). Courted by the GOP to oppose Bill Clinton in 1996, he passed.

CYNTHIA JOHNSON / TIME

END OF A SCOURGE

In April 1955, Dr. Jonas Salk, 40, of Pittsburgh injected a schoolboy with his newly approved vaccine against the highly communicable disease polio. It was the culmination of eight years of research and field trials (first human guinea pig: himself). Salk's dead-virus vaccine, as well as Alfred Sabin's more effective live-virus version, approved in 1960, virtually eradicated the childhood scourge.

ALBERT FENN / LIFE

FAMILIAR YET SO NEW

The New York art world was in thrall to abstract expressionism when a Georgian hit town. In 1954, Jasper Johns, 24 (an admirer of Dadaist Marcel Duchamp), began to make deadpan paintings of common icons: the Stars and Stripes, targets, even numbers. A smash 1958 gallery show helped pave the road to Pop Art. In 1999, a Johns fetched $7.1 million at auction.

PETER STACKPOLE / LIFE

A RACE AGAINST TIME

Even Roger Bannister, a medical student as well as a premier British miler, wondered if the human body was built to run that distance in less than four minutes. But on May 6, 1954, the future neurologist, 25, became the first, breaking the tape in 3:59.4.

MADE FIRST IN JAPAN

In 1954's *The Seven Samurai* (co-starring Toshiro Mifune, right), feudal warriors save a rural village. The balletic battles staged by director Akira Kurosawa, 44, were soon copied. The plot, too (as *The Magnificent Seven*). A later Kurosawa picture became the spaghetti Western that made Clint Eastwood; yet another inspired George Lucas to create Princess Leia and droids R2D2 and C3PO.

ARC DE GRAND MAC

Why were the owners of a single San Bernardino, California, drive-in (left) ordering so many milkshake makers from him? Ray Kroc, 52, flew out in 1954 to learn that the McDonald brothers — Richard, 45, and Maurice, 52 — were franchising their innovative fast-food techniques. An impressed Kroc bought in and later paid the burger kings $2.7 million for all rights.

CRISIS AT SUEZ

In Port Said, on the 100-mile-long Suez Canal, a British soldier inspected a cache of captured Egyptian munitions. Three months earlier, Egypt's Gamal Abdel Nasser had seized the internationally run waterway. On October 29, 1956, Britain joined France and Israel in an attack to win it back. Their victory was short-lived. A month later, the U.S. and USSR, in a rare Cold War accord, backed sending in a U.N. police force to clear the canal zone of combatants.

>
CRISIS IN HUNGARY

The world's eyes were on Suez when, on November 4, 1956, Moscow rolled 2,500 tanks (above right) and 120,000 troops into Budapest. Hungarians, hoping to evict their Soviet overlords, had recently decapitated a statue of Stalin in their capital. Now they not only fought their invaders but also executed members of the hated secret police (right). The outgunned freedom fighters took a reported 10,000 casualties before giving in. The U.S., needing Soviet cooperation in the Middle East, did not intervene.

UNCHAINED MELODIES

Alan Freed (here in 1959, at 33) is the man to laud — or damn — for midwifing the sound that swept the world. In 1951, while disc jockeying at a radio station in Cleveland, he began to spin 45s cut by rhythm-and-blues artists. His mostly white audience did not protest what was then called "race music." Freed gave it a more upbeat name, with help from the title of a 1947 R&B song by Wild Bill Moore ("We're Gonna Rock, We're Gonna Roll").

COSTA MANOS / MAGNUM

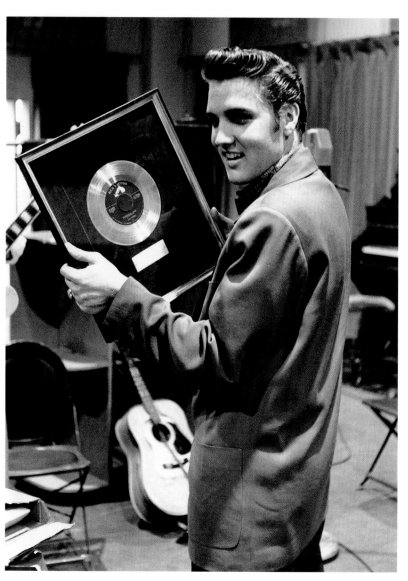

ROLL OVER, BEETHOVEN

The backbeat-driven sound sure riled the geezers, but there was more to it than that. Rock and roll had a musical inevitability. Back in 1947, Les Paul had taken a perfectly good guitar and stuck a cord in it. R&B had been Freed into white mainstream culture. But not until a movie director showcased a failed two-year-old single did rock reach critical mass. The movie: 1955's *Blackboard Jungle*, about juvenile delinquents. The song: "(We're Gonna) Rock Around the Clock" by Bill Haley and His Comets (above near left). The next year, Elvis Aron Presley, 21, of Tupelo, Mississippi, went gold with "Heartbreak Hotel" (left). The talented but haunted singer (older twin Jesse Garon was stillborn) redefined idolatry. In 1957, when Dick Clark, then 28, launched *American Bandstand* on national TV, not all chart toppers were rock (right). Soon they were. Clark continued on in an industry that — like Dorian Gray and some warhorse acts — would refuse to age.

TOP NEAR LEFT:
CORBIS / BETTMANN-UPI
LEFT: DON CRAVENS / LIFE
RIGHT: PAUL SCHUTZER / LIFE

COURTING GREATNESS

Surely, growing up in
Harlem, Althea Gibson
never expected to be feted
with a ticker tape parade
downtown. But in 1957, at
29, she had just become
the first black to win a
major singles tennis title,
the Wimbledon. (Nine
weeks later, Gibson added
the U.S. Nationals, now the
Open, crown.) By the time
the pro tour took root in the
late 1960s, alas, her game
was past its prime.

CORBIS / BETTMANN-UPI

BEFORE THE FALL

She went from nude calen-
dars to Hollywood B-icon:
the breathless, brainless
blonde whom gentlemen
preferred. Marilyn Monroe
sought more. In choicer
roles, as in 1959's *Some
Like It Hot*, she proved
herself one funny lady.
Personal happiness was
harder. After marriages to,
among others, Joe
DiMaggio and playwright
Arthur Miller (here, in
1956), she entered hapless
affairs with, among others,
JFK before OD'ing on drugs
in 1962, at age 36.

PAUL SCHUTZER / LIFE

BRICK BY BRICK

In August 1961, GIs and East German troops confronted each other across the crude wall being built by the Communists to bisect Berlin. Reason: Too many East Germans were fleeing to the West via the Allied-run sector of this partitioned city. The Wall was an instant Iron Curtain icon; in 1963, it played a key role in John le Carre's breakthrough thriller, *The Spy Who Came In from the Cold.*

PAUL SCHUTZER / LIFE

A COUNTRY'S REVENGE

A year earlier, the man in the glass booth had been at liberty in Argentina. Now, in 1961, Adolf Eichmann, 55 (with headset, left), sat in a Jerusalem court facing charges of genocide. His kidnapping had drawn global criticism, which Israel ignored. Eichmann, overseer of Hitler's extermination of Europe's Jews, was judged guilty and hanged the following May.

GJON MILI / LIFE

THE HIGH FRONTIER

The first human in space: Soviet cosmonaut Yuri Gagarin, 27 (left), two days after his April 12, 1961, mission. Welcoming him in Moscow was Nikita Khrushchev (as future premier Leonid Brezhnev, 54, hovered in the background). Gagarin's craft, *Vostok I*, hit 17,400 mph on the 89-minute flight. That May 5, astronaut Alan Shepard Jr., 37 (inset), became the first American in space. He rode *Freedom 7* to an altitude of 115 miles but did not orbit the planet, as had Gagarin. Although the U.S. was playing catch-up, JFK boldly vowed to put an American on the moon by the end of the decade.

JAMES WHITMORE / *LIFE*
INSET: NASA

273

A RECIPE FOR SAUSAGE

During Ike's last, lame-duck months, his CIA set up covert camps (mostly in Florida, right) to train anti-Castro exiles yearning to reclaim Cuba. An invasion date was set. JFK had been in the Oval Office less than three months when he reluctantly green-lighted the strike (while vetoing U.S. air support). On April 17, 1961, 1,500 paramilitants waded ashore at the Bay of Pigs. Three days later, 400 were dead and the rest captured (above). Castro, until then a professed anti-imperialist, declared himself a Communist.

ABOVE:
DOCUMENTATION ROGER PIC
RIGHT: LYNN PELHAM / LIFE

DESTINATION: CUBA. COURSE: COLLISION

At their first summit, in 1961 in Vienna, Soviet premier Nikita Khrushchev judged John F. Kennedy to be weak. The next summer, he began arming new ally Fidel Castro with medium-range ballistic missiles. On October 14, a U.S. spy plane photographed launch sites under construction. On the 22nd, JFK ordered an air and sea quarantine of Cuba. It took six days of angry negotiations, by way of intermediaries, letters and telexes, before Khrushchev caved and agreed to take back the weapons. (A Soviet freighter carrying home missiles was escorted by a U.S. warship, below.) Shaken by their close brush with nuclear war, the superpowers, in 1963, installed a hot line between Moscow and Washington.

RIGHT: ARTHUR RICKERBY / LIFE; BELOW: CARL MYDANS / LIFE

INVISIBLE TERRORS

Biologist Rachel Carson could also write; witness *The Sea Around Us*, her 1951 best-seller. Ten years later, at 54 (above), she finished another book. It eloquently examined how pesticides like DDT, in use only since the 1940s, were contaminating the food chain. *Silent Spring* led to a U.S. ban on most uses of DDT in 1972, eight years after Carson's death. It also sparked a global rethinking of man's place in the ecological scheme.

ALFRED EISENSTAEDT / LIFE

BUT THE MODEL WAS CHEAP

Cezanne painted a wine bottle, and no one blinked. Yet people howled at the canvases of Andy Warhol (right, painted in 1963, when the Pittsburgh native was 35). That many of his works seemed straight out of a supermarket flyer was precisely the point; if nothing else, Pop Art was fueled by artistic irony.

THE ANDY WARHOL FOUNDATION / ART RESOURCE

A TRAGIC RUSH TO MARKET

The German girl at right was born armless because of a sedative, popular in Europe, taken by her pregnant mother. But thalidomide never made it to the U.S. The FDA, for want of key test data, kept rejecting the drug until its side effects were clear (from 1959 on, 3,000-plus babies with defects in Germany and Great Britain).

STAN WAYMAN / LIFE

>

TWO EMANCIPATORS

Enfranchisement was not the same as emancipation, argued 42-year-old writer turned housewife Betty Friedan in her 1963 best-seller, *The Feminine Mystique*. It joined 1949's *The Second Sex*, by French existentialist Simone de Beauvoir, in rejecting the notion that biology was destiny — and thus mothered America's Women's Lib movement.

STEVE SCHAPIRO / LIAISON

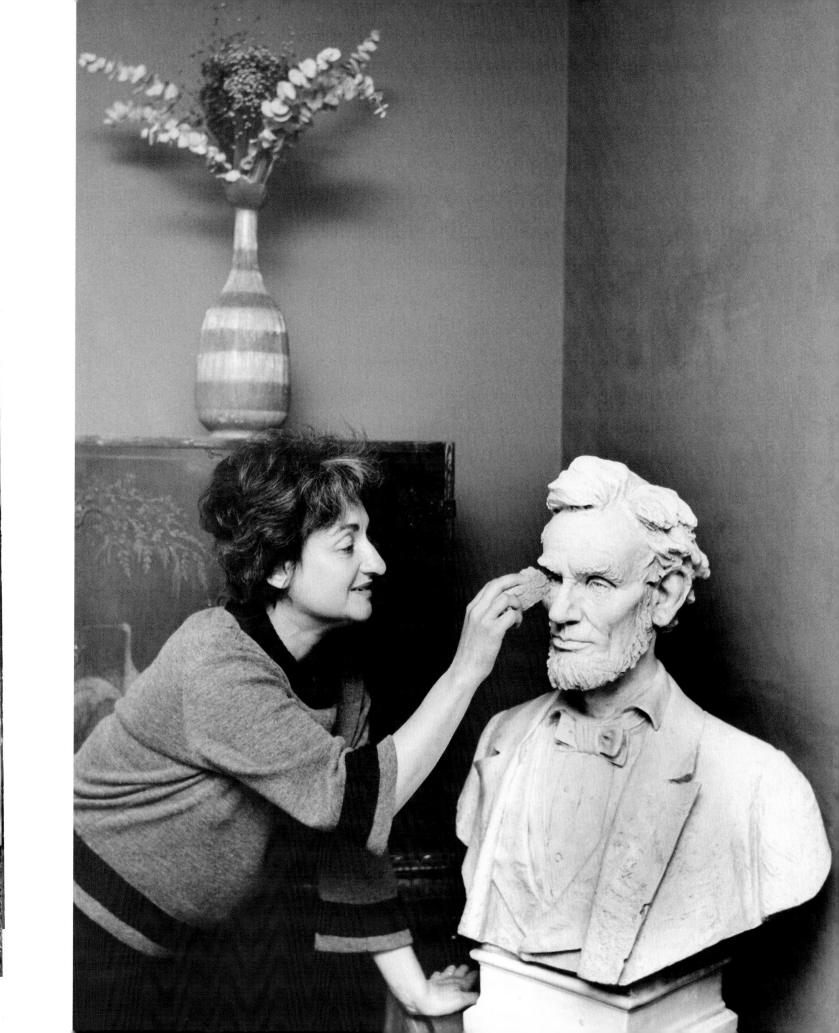

HE WILL BURY WHO?

A mote got into Nikita Khrushchev's eye in October 1964. Days later, it was a stick; the Kremlin ousted its premier after six years both turbulent (the Cuban missile crisis) and buffoonish (at a U.N. meeting, he banged on the desk with one of his shoes). Yet Khrushchev, 70, was the first Soviet leader to leave office alive. He and wife Nina finished their days at a dacha near Moscow.

HENRI DAUMAN

ACHTUNG! WAR IS FUNNY!

Peter Sellers's Dr. Strange-love, title character of the 1964 Stanley Kubrick Cold War satire, is a German now advising the Pentagon ("He's *our* Nazi"). This lampoon of the nuclear arms race is not subtle; other characters are named Merkin Muffley (also played by Sellers), Buck Turgidson, Bat Guano. But it did uncork a considerable supply of precious bodily fluids — tears of laughter.

ARCHIVE PHOTOS

THE MOUTH THAT ROARED

By KO'ing Sonny Liston in March 1964 (below), Cassius Clay became, at 22, world heavyweight champ. Soon he embraced the Black Muslim faith and adopted the name Muhammad Ali. But in 1967, upon refusing to be drafted, Ali was stripped of the title. He had to sit out three years. Not until 1974 did he reclaim the crown, by rope-a-doping George Foreman in the "Rumble in the Jungle" in Zaire.

HERB SCHARFMAN / LIFE

THE DAY BINGO DIED

On September 12, 1964, beverage distributor Paul Cardone (and wife Martha) of Gloversville, New York, hit a $100,000 jackpot in a neighboring state. Cost of ticket: three bucks. New Hampshire cleared $5.7 million from America's first legal lottery. By 1999, 37 states were conducting such drawings.

STEVE SCHAPIRO / LIFE

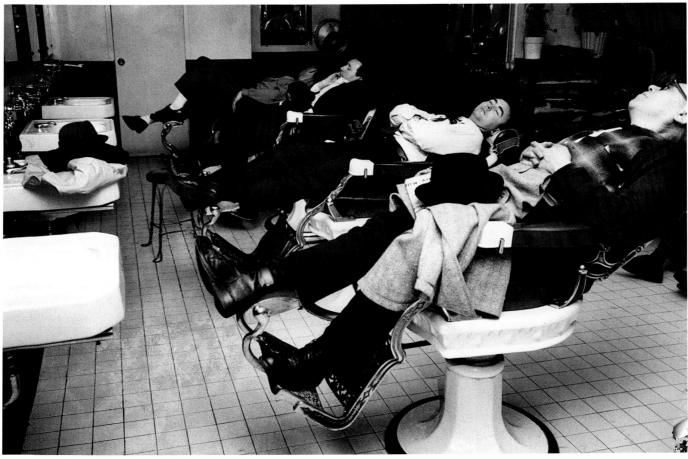

APOCALYPSE 1968

PARKING BY PERMIT ONLY

The Soviet tanks lining a Prague street in August were a harsh reality check for Czechoslovaks. Earlier in the year, their party boss, Alexander Dubček, 46, had bravely talked of nurturing a "socialism with a human face." Those words did not sit well with Moscow. On August 20, Warsaw Pact troops numbering 200,000 swept in to snuff out the liberalization movement known as Prague Spring.

BILL RAY / LIFE

HEADBANGERS BALL

John Evans of NBC News ignored his injuries to take notes; the August Democratic National Convention did not lack for stories. Delegates still reeling from LBJ's decision to quit arrived in a Chicago girded for war. Mayor Richard Daley, fearing Yippies would spike city reservoirs with LSD, had his cops in full riot mode. So for five days, they beat up not only young longhairs but also journalists, even ones on the convention floor.

CHICAGO SUN TIMES

TWO V'S FOR VICTORY

His body language was typically ungainly, but at an October GOP rally in Ohio, that trademark salute of Richard Nixon's seemed justified. He was pledging "peace with honor" in Vietnam and law and order at home. Further, his opponent, Vice President Hubert Humphrey, was tarred by the Democratic debacle in Chicago. Nixon sensed the prize was his. He was right.

WALTER BENNETT / TIME

> **THE NEW MUCKRAKERS**

The young lawyers on the House steps in 1969 were members of a firm recently founded by Ralph Nader, 35 (foreground). Its mission: ferret out suspect corporate practices like failing to correct the bad auto design exposed in Nader's 1965 *Unsafe at Any Speed*. An angered GM tried to smear the author; caught, it paid up. Nader used the $284,000 to help fund his Raiders.

JOHN ZIMMERMAN / LIFE

< **WELL, FLICK MY BIC**

Jimi showed. So did Baez. And Santana. And Grace and the Airplane. And Janis, 26 (inset), with *Bobby McGee*. They came in August 1969 to Max Yasgur's farm in Bethel, New York, 60 miles from Woodstock. In renting out his spread, Yasgur, 49, expected "three days of peace and music" — not a circus of the naked and the dead-to-the-world (from drugs). Some 300,000 attended. Many more now say they did.

JOHN DOMINIS / LIFE
INSET: HENRY DILTZ /
CORBIS / BETTMANN

> **SEND IN THE CLOWNS**

Betting their bippies that vaudeville was not dead, Judy Carne, 29 (near right), Goldie Hawn, 22, and Chelsea Brown, 21, became resident ding-a-lings on 1968's NBC show *Laugh-In*. The show recycled shtick without shame (here come de judge; sock it to me; knock-knock, who's there?). Yes, five of six gags were groaners. But in prime time, a laff a minute ain't bad.

TRANSWORLD FEATURE SYNDICATE

<
MISSION: POSSIBLE

On July 20, 1969, just five months short of the target date set eight years earlier by JFK, Neil Armstrong, 38 (left), of Wapakoneta, Ohio, stepped from the *Apollo 11* lander onto the surface of the moon, followed by Buzz Aldrin, 39, of Montclair, New Jersey. Said Armstrong, "That's one small step for man, one giant leap for mankind." Indeed.

NASA

TURNING POINT:
EXPLORING THE HEAVENS

Upward Mobility

Sputnik I broke free of earth before two-thirds of all Americans now alive were born. Perhaps that is why the twinkles in the night sky awe us less than they did our forebears. Manned missions go unnoted unless their peril is brought tragically home. Unmanned missions? Snore. Yet it is the high-tech drones that have stretched the bandwidth of astronomical data. For example, we now know the universe has expanded since the Big Bang 13 billion years ago, has no boundary and may, or may not, contract. (Probably not.) But all we have learned in a historical eye blink still leaves unanswered the most vexing question: Within the vast firmament beginning where our atmosphere ends, do any other beings dwell? At cosmology's door rightly meet science and religion.

... LIKE A BIG PIZZA PIE

Tout Paris roared in 1902 at the finale (left) of the first sci-fi flick. In 1895, Georges Méliès, 34, had caught the first film by *les frères* Lumière (see page 282). A magician by trade, he drew on his craft to invent cinematic narrative. The 14-minute, 30-scene *A Trip to the Moon*, loosely drawn from an 1865 Jules Verne novel, was one of his 400-plus short works.

CULVER PICTURES

> HAIL, NOT HEIL!

More than his arm was in a sling when Wernher Von Braun, 33 (right), gave up to GIs in 1945. The Nazi rocket scientist had upgraded the Vergeltungswaffen-1 (Revenge Missile-1) into the more lethal, 13-ton V-2 (inset) that creamed Britain late in World War II. Braun cut a deal with the U.S., though (as did other Germans with the USSR), and ended up a NASA bigwig. A biography titled *Reaching for the Stars* was fast subtitled, by skeptics, *(And Hitting London)*.

U.S. ARMY (2)

< A BABY STEP INTO SPACE

He was so sure about his notions for a propulsion system to come that in 1914, at 32, Robert Goddard filed two patents. A prototype liquid-fueled rocket (left) was eventually built. On March 16, 1926, in Auburn, Massachusetts, Goddard ignited it. The device rose 41 feet into the air. Space was suddenly much closer.

SMITHSONIAN INSTITUTION

WE'RE NO. 1!

Muscovites in late 1957 were agog at a replica of *Sputnik I*, but think how miserable America's military and scientific elite felt. The 184-pound Soviet satellite was shot into orbit that October 4. It fell back into earth's atmosphere on January 4, 1958, and burned to a crisp.

ARCHIVE PHOTOS

THE ORIGINAL RIGHT STUFF

After sifting through 508 applicants for Project Mercury (its expedited program to send a man into space), the six-month-old National Aeronautics and Space Administration in 1959 announced the chosen seven, whom it dubbed "astronauts." They were, clockwise from top left, Alan Shepard, Gus Grissom, Gordon Cooper, Scott Carpenter, John Glenn, Deke Slayton and Wally Schirra. All would make it off planet.

RALPH MORSE / TIME

FIRST TICKET TO RIDE

Crack Soviet parachutist Valentina Tereshkova, 26, went in the opposite direction on June 16, 1963, aboard *Vostok 6* and was thus the first woman and 10th human to orbit earth (48 times over three days). She later married a fellow cosmonaut, Andriyan Nikolayev. The couple had one daughter.

SOVFOTO / TASS

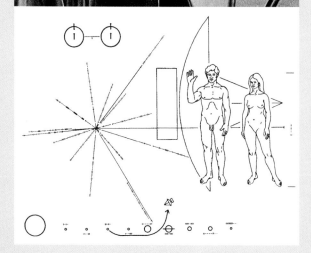

IF U CN RD THS MSG

Affixed to the skin of the space probe *Pioneer 10* is the gold-oxidized aluminum plate pictured at left. Its sign language reveals where, when and by whom the craft was launched. On June 13, 1983, 11 years and three months after leaving earth, *Pioneer 10* passed Pluto's orbit. So far the first man-made object to leave the solar system has not been returned to sender.

NASA

NASA RECYCLES

The launch of *Columbia* on April 12, 1981 — and its pilot-controlled landing back at Cape Canaveral 54 hours later — was to have opened a new era of space exploration. With a shuttle fleet that would grow to four, NASA hoped to run a mission a month. But the vehicles needed longer than planned in turnaround; it took 57 months to send up the first two dozen. On flight 10, astronauts Bruce McCandless (inset) and Robert Stewart, using newly developed jet backpacks, became the first to take an untethered spacewalk.

CHARLES TRAINOR / MIAMI NEWS
INSET: NASA

ERRORS WERE MADE

Spring 1975. The situation in Vietnam was worsening. This evac flight out of provincial capital Nha Trang was overloaded. The pilot had to slug a latecomer who would not take no for an answer. The undeclared war killed some three million Vietnamese and, officially, 58,000 American service personnel. The psychic damages are still being measured.

THAI KNAO CHUON /
CORBIS / BETTMANN-UPI

A PEACEFUL TRANSITION

On August 9, 1974, Richard Nixon, 61, shrugged his last presidential salute (inset). Veep Gerald Ford, 61, and his wife, Betty, 56, went back to the White House to wait. Some 90 minutes later, by way of a presigned letter, Nixon became the only U.S. chief executive to resign (to avoid impeachment for his role in the Watergate coverup). At 12:03 p.m., Ford was sworn in as the 38th president. He soon pardoned Nixon; it would cost him his job in 1976.

DENNIS BRACK / BLACK STAR
INSET: BILL PIERCE / TIME

COMEDY ISN'T PRETTY

ABC had just launched a prime-time hour called *Saturday Night Live with Howard Cosell*, so in October 1975, a rival network called its 90-minute after-hours satirical revue *NBC's Saturday Night* — airing "Live! From New York. . . ." The gags were sometimes lame but not the charter troupe: counterclockwise from near right, Chevy Chase, 32; John Belushi, 26; Garrett Morris, 38; Laraine Newman, 23; Jane Curtin, 28; Dan Aykroyd, 23; and Gilda Radner, 29. They all live yet in reruns. Enjoy.

FOTO FANTASIES

REQUIEM

> **ROBERTO CLEMENTE
1934–1972**

He turned Pittsburgh's hapless Pirates into contenders and, twice, world champs. Three months after collecting his 3,000th (and last) hit, he flew on a mercy mission to earthquake-torn Nicaragua. The plane crashed. Baseball waived its five-year-wait rule to make Clemente the first Hall of Famer from Puerto Rico.

AL SATTERWHITE

<

MARGARET BOURKE-WHITE, 1904–1971

The charter *Life* staffer took risks to cover combat; her transport to North Africa in 1942 was torpedoed and sunk. She also trained her eye on Southern poverty, the liberation of Nazi death camps and Gandhi's campaign to free India. Bourke-White's images helped define the new art of photojournalism.

MARGARET BOURKE-WHITE / LIFE

>

**COLE PORTER
1891–1964**

Driven by lyrics both erudite and witty ("You're an O'Neill drama; you're Whistler's mama"), his tunes hooked both the café set and Middle America. A 1937 riding fall crippled Porter but not his career; he worked from bed, even staging musical tryouts (right). The last of his 20 Broadway shows was 1955's *Silk Stockings*.

GEORGE KARGER / LIFE

ERNESTO (CHE) GUEVARA
1928–1967

He was the original rebel without a pause. An Argentine of Spanish and Irish descent (one grandmother was a U.S. citizen), he forsook a medical career to foment revolution in five countries. In 1956, Guevara hooked up with Fidel Castro; Cuba was to be his only winner. His last guerrilla campaign was in Bolivia. The CIA found him, the Bolivians shot him.

LEE LOCKWOOD / TIME INC.

WOODY GUTHRIE
1912–1967

Saloons and hobo camps were favorite haunts of the one-man protest band (and paradigm for Sixties folksingers like son Arlo and Bob Dylan). Of his 1,000-plus songs, the best known is "This Land Is Your Land." It was later used in upbeat advertising campaigns. Funny; Woody wrote it to condemn the ownership of private property.

ERIC SCHAAL / LIFE

On turning 200, these United States of
America numbered 50 (from 13), and its
218 million citizens (from 2.5 million) spoke
350-plus tongues (from a handful).

J.P. LAFFONT / SYGMA

1976–1992

A GLOBAL BURST OF FREEDOM

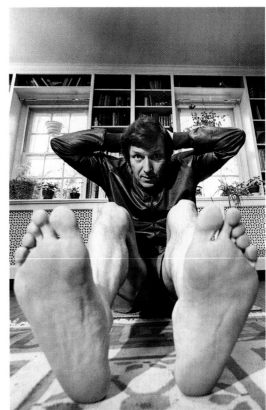

DISTURBING THE FIELD

O.K., so the desert was in
Tunisia, not on the planet
Tatooine in a galaxy far, far
away. And those droids
were actually British actors
Anthony Daniels, 30 (left),
and Kenny Baker, 41. Still,
we suspended disbelief
over 1977's *Star Wars*,
filmed by director George
Lucas, 33, for $7.8 million.
The fifth (of nine) episodes
of the saga that changed
not only Hollywood but also
pop culture is due in
theaters May 19, 2002.

LUCASFILMS

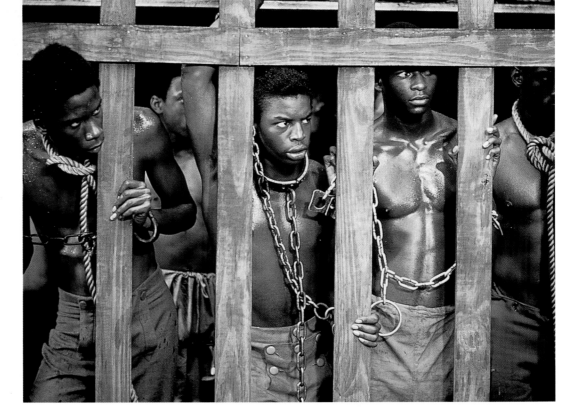

BUMP AND RUN

A tangle late in the 3,000 meters (between America's falling Mary Decker, 26, and barefoot Zola Budd, 18, running for Britain) was a rare glitch at the 1984 Los Angeles Olympics. They were the first Games to turn a nice profit. And with the USSR saying *nyet* — tit-for-tatting America's boycott of 1980's Moscow Games — Team USA won a national-best 174 medals.

DAVID BURNETT / CONTACT

<

LOVE AMONG THE RUINS

The bridal couple threading through the Beirut rubble symbolized the Lebanese city once a gem of the Mediterranean; they were crossing the Green Line that split his Muslim sector from an altar in her Christian sector. In 1982 Ronald Reagan sent U.S. Marines to the city to keep the peace. On October 23, 1983, their barracks was truck-bombed (inset), with a death toll of 241.

JAY ULLAL / BLACK STAR
INSET: BILL FOLEY / AP

HEAR ME ROAR

In July 1984, Martina Navratilova, 27, scorched Wimbledon (right) as she had the French Open and would the U.S. Open. The Czech-born naturalized American was on the run of a lifetime: In one stretch of 20 Grand Slam events, she won 12. Wielding a serve-and-volley game rare for women's tennis, she retired in 1994 with 167 titles, most by any player. Any.

LEO MASON / SIPA

A RELUCTANT POSTER BOY

The 1985 announcement by actor Rock Hudson, 59, that he had AIDS led to greater public understanding and sympathy — and to safer sex and closer screening of blood supplies. The not-so-new epidemic (the first suspected case dates to 1959) peaked in the U.S. in 1993. But globally, the as-yet-incurable disease remains on the rise.

ALAIN VAN DE WALLE / LIAISON

EVEN HOPE DISAPPEARED

Starvation had taken her parents, so an Ethiopian girl awaited death at a make-shift orphanage (below). The 1984 famine, in the midst of a civil war, was not East Africa's first or last. It may have been the most tragic. Desperate images like this led to all-star rockathons and epic airlifts of food. Few relief supplies reached the victims; they were blocked by rival warlords.

DAVID BURNETT / CONTACT

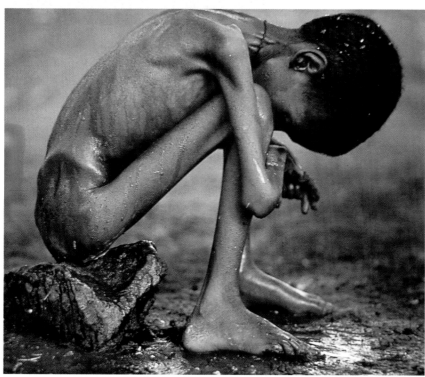

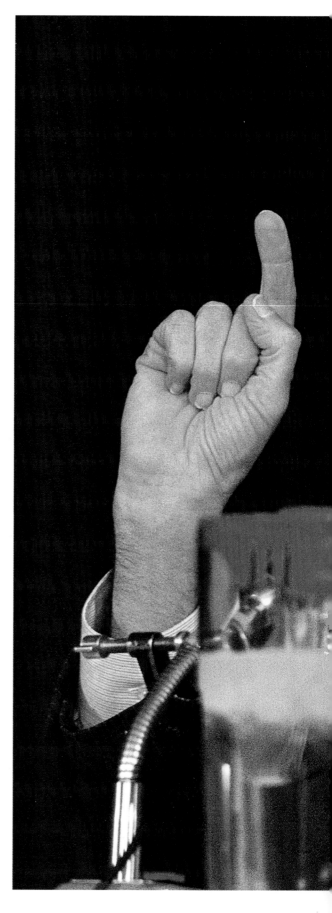

CUTTING TO THE CHASE

A disaster like *Challenger* (inset, the crew's NASA portrait) begs for answers; thus, 13 eminences were tapped to sit on 1986's blue-ribbon Rogers Commission, including Nobel physicist Richard Feynman, 67 (left). Witnesses agreed a booster-rocket gasket had failed, but not why. Suspecting that the abnormally cold temperature on launch day was a factor, Feynman ran a simple test on live TV. He dunked a strip of the rubbery gasket in a pitcher of ice water for one minute, then bent the now-stiffened O-ring material. It snapped.

DIANA WALKER / TIME
INSET: NASA

>

50 NEW WAR ZONES

In the decade and a half since *Roe* v. *Wade*, the debate on abortion had only intensified. Emerging pro-life groups such as Operation Rescue began picketing abortion clinics. Then in 1989, the Supreme Court gave states the right to enact abortion laws (subject to judicial review); soon, state capitals began to feel the heat.

DIANA WALKER / TIME

<

DEADLY QUID PRO QUO

The corpses at top left had been passengers on an Iran Air flight downed in July 1988 by missiles fired in error from USS *Vincennes*, on patrol in the Persian Gulf; 290 died. In December, 259 died on a Pan Am flight downed by a hidden bomb; the falling debris killed 11 villagers in Lockerbie, Scotland (below left). Claiming credit: several radical Islamic groups.

TOP LEFT: SIPA
BOTTOM LEFT:
STUART FRANKLIN / MAGNUM

>

COGITO ERGO SUM

Lou Gehrig's disease took English physicist Stephen Hawking's body. Yet he kept positing theories that led to an academic chair once held by Isaac Newton and, at 46 (right), published the 1988 best-seller *A Brief History of Time*. In 1999, Hawking agreed to be ribbed on *The Simpsons* — and even did his own (computer-generated) voice-over.

TERRY SMITH

HELLO, GOODBYE

A new world order was nigh in December 1988 as three presidents of two super-powers met in one place. To New York City's Governors Island went Mikhail Gorbachev, 57, in his 45th month as Kremlin head; Ronald Reagan, 77, in his 94th month in the White House; and George Bush, two months away from taking office.

DIRCK HALSTEAD / TIME

MAN OF STEELY NERVES

An indelible image from 1989: one lone Chinese against a column of T-59s in central Beijing (inset, right). More astonishing: his chat with the tank crew. Cordiality soon vanished. China's rulers wanted 100-acre Tiananmen Square cleared of a pro-democracy sit-in that began in mid-April. On June 4, the army went in. No body count has ever been released.

STUART FRANKLIN / MAGNUM (2)

IVAN WENT HOME

In May 1988, these troops were part of the first Soviet units to march out of Afghanistan. Moscow's death toll from nine years of warfare: 15,000. The Red Army's inability to crush the mujahedin damaged military morale, a fact noted in the West (and in Eastern Europe). Afghanistan would later erupt in a civil war won in 1996 by the ultra-fundamentalist Taliban.

ANDY HERNANDEZ / LIAISON

> **DEATH BE NOT PROUD**

Jack Kevorkian's IV drip was first tested in June 1990 by an Alzheimer's victim. It worked: The potassium chloride killed her. The assisted suicide renewed a euthanasia debate already complicated by medical technology: When is it O.K. to unplug? In 1999, after Kevorkian, by then 70, had assisted in 130-plus deaths, a jury finally convicted him of second-degree murder.

AP

> **BAD NEWS, GOOD NEWS**

Nature designed an otter's fur to repel seawater, but this one was in Prince William Sound, Alaska, in 1989, after the tanker *Exxon Valdez* ran aground and leaked some 11 million gallons of oil. Wildlife beyond count died, some colonies forever. Yet predictions of long-term disaster overlooked the fact that the Sound had recouped from another major ecodisaster, the earthquake of 1964.

TONY DAWSON

< **SCRAP-IRON CURTAIN**

East Berlin guards would normally have used rifles, not water jets, on the West German savaging the Wall. But it was November 1989, and 160 million people in five nations had said to their Soviet overlords, Enough. First to bolt, in August, was Poland, followed by Hungary, East Germany, Bulgaria, Czechoslovakia and Romania. Moscow, drained by Afghanistan, did not intervene.

TONY SUAU / LIAISON

< **WHOM DO YOU BELIEVE?**

Law professor Anita Hill, 35, testified reluctantly at the 1991 Senate hearings on Supreme Court nominee Clarence Thomas, 43. He was George Bush's pick to replace a fellow black, the retiring Thurgood Marshall. Hill gave accounts of lurid sexual harassment by former boss Thomas. She was vilified, he was confirmed (by 52–48, the tightest vote of the century).

SCOTT ANDERSEN / AP

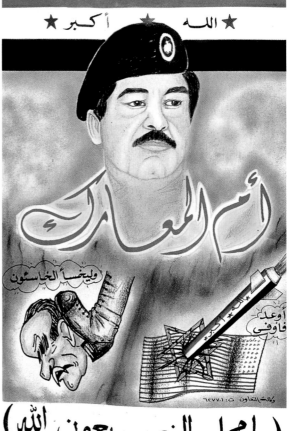

★ الله ★ اكبر ★

(يامحلى النصر بعون الله)

A Lopsided Duel in the Desert

The fastest route home was also the deadliest
(left) for Iraqis whose occupation of Kuwait
abruptly ended in late February 1991. Saddam
Hussein, their self-venerating president (above),
had made the mother of all miscalculations. His
country and its tiny neighbor (pop: 1.9 million,
only half native Kuwaitis) had long argued over
a shared oil field. Already praised by the U.S. for
his war with Iran, Hussein in mid-1990 got
official word that Washington didn't care about
Persian Gulf border disputes. He promptly
seized Kuwait. Whereupon 28 nations (nine of
them Arab states) formed a 690,000-strong
force led by U.S. general Norman Schwarzkopf,
56 (inset). Operation Desert Storm opened
with fierce air and missile attacks on Iraq.
On February 23, the ground campaign began.
It took 100 hours to clear Kuwait of Iraqis. But
the drive stopped short of Baghdad, leaving
Hussein, 53, still in dictatorial power.

LEFT: DENNIS BRACK / BLACK STAR
ABOVE: ALEXIS DUCIOS / LIAISON
INSET: HARRY BENSON

DOUBLE JEOPARDY

It was a case of same song, different verse in Los Angeles in 1991. Early on March 3, cops were right to bust the driver who had led them on a high-speed chase — but not with their nightsticks, boots and stun guns. An onlooker taped the attack and gave his sickening footage (above) to a local TV station. In days, the brutalized victim, Rodney King, a 25-year-old laborer (inset), became the symbol of the LAPD's callous treatment of minorities. Four white officers were put on trial. Their acquittal a year later, by an all-white suburban jury, inflamed the city's heavily black South-Central district (right). The riot ran for two days. Its toll: 50-plus dead, 2,000-plus injured, 12,000 arrested, $1 billion in damages and a racial polarization that would soon become evident in the murder trial of O.J. Simpson.

SCOTT WEERSING / LIAISON
ABOVE: GEORGE HOLIDAY / KTLA-TV

<

THE BEAR TAMER

On May 29, 1990, Boris Yeltsin, 59, became president of Russia — and thus No. 2 man to Gorbachev in a USSR on life-support. Its Eastern European empire was gone, and member republics were seceding. In August 1991, Kremlin die-hards tried a coup. Yeltsin heroically intervened; then, after parliament shuttered the Communist Party, he got Gorbachev to dissolve the Soviet Union itself.

AP

>

OUT OF THE OZARKS

The Bush Administration was still basking in Desert Storm's patriotic glow when from the mosh pit of 1992 Democratic long-shots and no-names rose Bill Clinton. Hadn't the Arkansas governor, 45, already fessed up in prime time to a less than perfect marriage? And didn't his staff fear another bimbo eruption? The White House surely anticipated Dukakis II.

CYNTHIA JOHNSON / TIME

<

A FUNNY THING . . .

. . . happened on the way to Election Day, 1992: Ross Perot, 62 (and, as ever, on *Larry King Live!*). The Texas data-processing mogul, mad at George Bush over Vietnam MIAs, check-booked himself into the race and fragged the president. The U.S. economy soured. The Rodney King case verdicts rocked Los Angeles. More of Perot's 19.7 million votes came from disaffected Republicans than from Democrats.

SHELLY KATZ / LIAISON

REQUIEM

GEORGIA O'KEEFFE
1887–1986

Her earliest works were abstracts, but by the time other American painters embraced the school, she had moved on to her signature series of oversized flowers. O'Keeffe resettled in New Mexico in the 1940s. There, her startlingly sensual vision turned austere and haunting: The late canvases are often of desert-scoured skulls.

DAVID GAHR

<

VLADIMIR NABOKOV
1899–1977

A Russian aristocrat uprooted by revolution, he lived mostly in boarding-houses and fraying hotels. Nabokov wrote 10 novels in his native tongue before switching to English. The success of 1958's *Lolita*, a riotous tale of ruinous obsession, meant more leisure to pursue his own passion: butterflies.

CARL MYDANS / LIFE

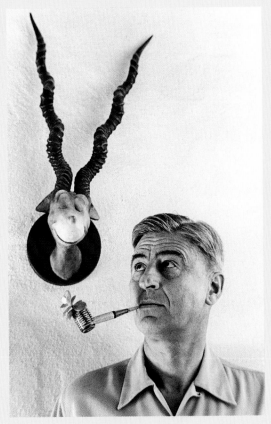

DOCTOR SEUSS
1904–1991

Theodor Geisel won honors for writing ads and World War II documentaries. Then he won fame and fortune for writing (and illustrating) 47 books for children of all ages. The blue-green abelard at right was one of his whimsical chimeras; another was a cat in a hat.

JOHN BRYSON

BOB MARLEY
1945–1981

When "I Shot the Sheriff" was covered by a Brit (Eric Clapton), the curious sought out the artist whose song it was. By then, of course, Marley was already a legend in his native Jamaica. His Rastafarian dreadlocks and enjoyment of ganja played as well off-island as his reggae. A political activist to boot, he survived a 1976 assault but not cancer.

RICHARD CREAMER / RETNA, LTD.

BING CROSBY
1903–1977

He cloaked his personal demons behind an insouciant stage manner and a croon that mellowed America. Crosby took his act from nightclubs to radio to movies (most famously, seven *Road* flicks with Bob Hope) to TV. One of the few to be a headliner in five decades, his voice will always make Christmas cheery and bright.

JOHNNY FLOREA / LIFE

GRETA GARBO
1905–1990

No, she never portrayed Catherine the Great (but did play Anna Karenina). It was news when Garbo talked (1930's *Anna Christie*). And laughed (1939's *Ninotchka*). And fled (1941, after 25 Hollywood roles). The enigmatic Swede spent the rest of her years roaming Manhattan's Upper East Side in disguises that fooled no one.

MGM

MARIA CALLAS
1923–1977

Her high-octane portrayals of tragic heroines revived neglected repertory at opera houses around the world. But the U.S.-born diva's penchant for off-stage melodrama (sudden cancellations, a public dumping by Aristotle Onassis for the widowed Jackie Kennedy) undid her career. Only a fatal heart attack kept Callas from writing her tell-all memoirs.

ELIOT ELISOFON / LIFE

LEONARD BERNSTEIN
1918–1990

In 1943, he was called in to lead the New York Philharmonic without rehearsal. His brilliant debut propelled the American conductor onto podiums here — as well as in Europe, reversing decades of tradition. Long-haired but not stuffy, Bernstein hosted TV specials to attract kids to classical music and also composed for the masses (including *West Side Story*).

HENRY GROSSMAN

FRED ASTAIRE
1899–1987

Despite enough custom size-eight-and-a-halfs to choke a clotheshorse, those tootsies got hot. Their owner danced through 33 Hollywood musicals, notably 10 opposite Ginger Rogers. If genius is 90 percent perspiration, Astaire never let us see the sweat as he revolutionized the art of hoofing and redefined our image of gentlemanly sophistication.

BOB LANDRY / LIFE

>
TENNESSEE WILLIAMS
1911–1983

He loaded his dramas with faded belles, cripples and brutes from the Deep South, but their tortured search for happiness and forgiveness is universal. In just 11 years, Williams (born in Mississippi) wrote *The Glass Menagerie*, *A Streetcar Named Desire* and *Cat on a Hot Tin Roof*. Booze and drugs were his downfall; he choked to death on a medicine-bottle cap.

W. EUGENE SMITH / LIFE

GEORGE BALANCHINE
1904–1983

One of the last dancers schooled under the czars — and, in 1924, one of the first to defect from the USSR — he originally worked in Paris with Diaghelev. Balanchine came to the U.S. in 1934. At the New York City Ballet, the imperious Mr. B choreographed a repertoire of plotless pieces that jetéd classical ballet forward into the 20th Century.

MARTHA SWOPE / TIME INC.

MARGARET MEAD
1901–1978

Never one to succumb to mynah distractions, Mead began her anthropological career at age eight by studying her sisters' speech. In the mid-1920s, she lived with natives on Samoa and New Guinea; they inspired her revolutionary thesis that sex roles are determined by culture. Mead's lack of supporting data invited criticism, but not her zest for fieldwork.

CORBIS / BETTMANN

>
ALFRED HITCHCOCK
1899–1980

He framed his thrillers as races against the clock (or a ravening flock). He dragged out suspense like a gleeful psycho. He gave his heroes flaws not unlike his own, which owed to a vertiginously repressed youth. He treated actors like cattle, yet prodded, from some, career performances. But it was his trademark cameos that made each of his 53 movies a Hitchcock.

LISA LARSEN / LIFE

<
CHARLIE CHAPLIN
1889–1977

Surrealistic slapstick made the London-born comedian Hollywood's first global superstar; in the era of silents, who didn't understand the Little Tramp? Chaplin had no such luck in talkies. His growing left-wing sympathies (and continuing taste for teenage girls) led the U.S. to deny him reentry in 1952. The privilege was restored in 1973 so he could accept an honorary Oscar.

W. EUGENE SMITH / LIFE

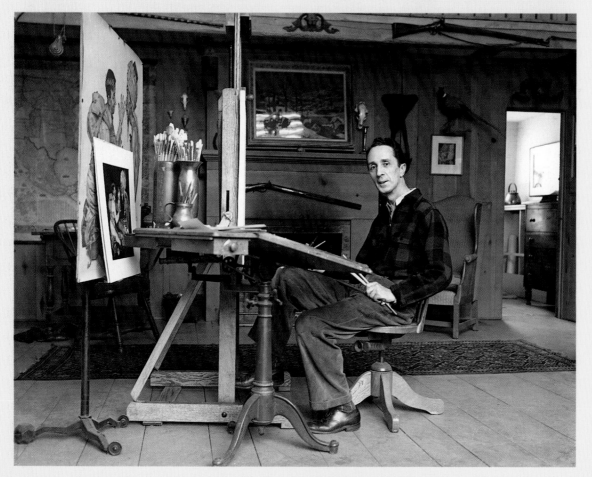

<
NORMAN ROCKWELL
1894–1978

Painting from life was de rigueur for the artist: The faces of neighbors routinely graced his signature *Saturday Evening Post* covers. Not all Rockwell's works were as saccharine as those Americana set pieces. In his last 14 years, he applied his precise brush to social issues like segregation's tragic costs.

AP

> **JIM HENSON**
1936–1990

Big Bird, Cookie and the grouchy Oscar belonged to *Sesame Street*, the PBS show that the innovative puppetmeister helped make must-watch kidvid. But the Muppets belonged to Henson, who Miss Piggy-backed them into a showbiz empire. Until his death (from a rare but treatable strep), he always found time to give voice to his alter ego, the gentle, wry Kermit T. Frog.

JIM HENSON COMPANY

JOHN WAYNE
1907–1979

It's a pity Gary Cooper beat him to the punch line: "If you want to call me that, smile." Wayne brooked no insubordination in his 250-plus movies (playing cowboys, soldiers, cops and even a Mongol, but never the villain). In 1955, he spurned a new CBS Western called *Gunsmoke*. Musta hadda hunch the tube was too danged small for him.

PHIL STERN / CPI

1993-1999

There was no silencing this lamb's creation in July 1996. Dolly, here on her first birthday, was from neither the union of ram and ewe nor a test tube; she was cloned by Scottish geneticist Ian Wilmut from a single cell of her mother.

And Now the News: Man Bytes Dogma

BY PAUL SAFFO

WELCOME TO THE decade of the dot, that tiny bit of Internet grammar whose ubiquity in E-mail addresses and Web URLs so neatly captures the giddying impact of technology on our lives at century's end.

Seven years ago, the Internet was little more than a cyberspace wilderness traversed by nerds and early adopters, while the Web was an obscure tool unknown to all but a handful of researchers. Today, the Internet is a more potent medium than television, and the Web is driving the Dow into the stratosphere as it reinvents one new industry after another.

If the dot is the Nineties' symbol, then the S-curve is its trajectory. This is the curve of Moore's law, which dictates that the number of circuits packed onto computer chips doubles every 18 months with the result that the power of the chips doubles at the same rate and their cost drops by half. It is why a Furby has several times the processing power carried on board the Apollo command module, and the latest generation of video-game players out-performs the best graphics supercomputers of a decade ago.

The S-curve is everywhere we look in this decade. It is the curve of traffic on the Internet, of transactions on the World Wide Web, of cellular phone sales and, at moments, of unread E-mail lurking in our in boxes. It is the curve of new scientific discoveries and also is the curve of our collective surprise and uncertainty as we struggle to understand the revolutions swirling around us. Thus, the ubiquitous dot is not merely a mark in cyberspace but also the anchor in the exclamation points and question marks punctuating our astonishment at all that is afoot.

Technology empowers. It floods our lives with options and overwhelms us with choice, and it places us squarely in the middle of the revolutions it generates. But with choice comes the burden of choosing wisely. Computers and E-mail can free us from the tyranny of rush hour or lure us into working 24 hours a

In this tiny Montana shack were built mail bombs — 16 in 17 years — that killed three, maimed 23. The Unabomber gave his technophobic rationale in a 1995 screed. His kid brother recognized the author's style. In 1998, Ted Kaczynski, 55, drew life times four.
RICHARD BARNES

day. Satellites and video can remind us that the world is indeed a global village or simply display a missile's eye view of warfare in real time. New wonder drugs can lower infant mortality or simply allow us to grow more hair, improve sexual performance and have litters of designer children.

Technology also changes our view of reality even when it does not touch us directly. This decade has seen one astonishing technology-enabled discovery after another. The Hubble telescope has reached deep into look-back time and reminded us that even "empty" corners of the sky are teeming with galaxies. Robots drift through the oceans, revealing unimagined geographies and discovering exotic life-forms that would have taxed the imagination of a science fiction writer a decade earlier. The universe keeps getting bigger, but so does our world, as we discover that this planet we live on is vastly more subtle and complex than we ever imagined.

"I'm all for progress; it's change I object to." That sentiment, expressed by Mark Twain a century ago, is echoed in our ambivalence toward technology and the life-changing choices it forces upon us. We complain about E-mail and phone calls, but we still rush out to buy the latest, smallest cell phone so that we are never out of touch. The *Titanic* disaster fascinates us as a tale of techno-hubris even as we are transfixed by the submarine robots that brought images of the wreck into our living rooms. And *Star*

Wars still works its magic as a morality tale about the battle between technologies that amplify the human spirit (Luke Skywalker) and technologies that extinguish it (Darth Vader).

Without a doubt, we have become steadily more dependent upon ever more complex and obscure technologies. In general, the less visible a computer is, the more important a role it plays in one's life. Smash my laptop, and I'll pull out a pen and paper and keep working. Crash the computer switch in the local phone exchange, and I am isolated. But mess with the computer running the power grid, and I'm thrown back to an age of candles and oil lamps with rotting food in the refrigerator.

The past two decades have been punctuated by reminders of the complexities — and cost — of our myriad technological choices. Techno-disasters from Chernobyl to Bhopal, from TWA Flight 800 to mad-cow disease, splash across the news. Technology undoubtedly is an amplifier, not just of our hopes, but also of our carelessness, our ignorance

DANGEROUS PEACE

Israeli prime minister Yitzhak Rabin, 71, did not hide his feelings at a 1993 photo op with Bill Clinton and PLO leader Yasir Arafat, 64. But he then shook hands on an accord to give Palestinians more autonomy. The next year, he signed a peace pact with Jordan. Sixteen months later, in Tel Aviv, Rabin was shot dead by a right-wing Israeli.

CYNTHIA JOHNSON / TIME

TALL TARGETS

Had the terrorist parked his rental truck closer to a girder in the garage below Manhattan's World Trade Center in February 1993, the blast would have killed far more than six and injured far more than 1,000. The hit was directed by Omar Abdul Rahman, 54, ex-adviser to Afghanistan's mujahedin (see page 349). The blind cleric hoped to topple one 110-story tower into its twin.

MARK CARDWELL / REUTERS / ARCHIVE PHOTOS

WHERE THERE'S SMOKE

In April 1994, eight corporate chiefs swore to Congress they were not merchants of menace. Though their mainstay product had been declared hazardous to humans by the U.S. Surgeon General 30 years earlier, the cigarette moguls insisted they had no personal knowledge of risks. Yet in 1997, their industry headed off a legion of lawsuits by coughing up $368.5 billion.

JOHN DURICKA / AP

>
BETRAYED BY BLOODLINES

Some 1.5 million fled the African nation of Rwanda in spring 1994 — this family to next-door Tanzania — when five centuries of tribal animosity between Hutus and Tutsis flared into another civil war. An estimated 500,000 were less fortunate: They died so brutally that in 1998, a U.N. tribunal found the nation's then prime minister guilty of genocide.

JOE ALEXANDER / AFP

SIC TRANSIT GLORIA

Newt Gingrich's prize for steering the GOP to congressional majorities in 1994: the House Speakership (and a *Time* Man of the Year cover the next year, here being photographed by Gregory Heisler). The ex-history teacher, 52, had correctly read the backlash against big-government Clinton proposals like health-care reform. In 1998, Gingrich was sure Monicagate made the lame-duck president a sitting duck as well. America disagreed. When the Republicans' edge was trimmed, the Speaker quit.

P.F. BENTLEY / TIME

PEACE IN THEIR TIME

Apartheid ended not with a
bang but with this salute. In
May 1994, Nelson Mandela,
75, was sworn in as South
Africa's president and his
predecessor, F.W. de Klerk,
58, as a deputy president.
Four years earlier, De Klerk
had freed Mandela after 27
years as a political prisoner.
Their subsequent dialogue
on black-white power
sharing won them a joint
Nobel — and their beloved
country a multiracial future.

JUDA NGWENYA / REUTERS /
ARCHIVE PHOTOS

IF THE GLOVE DOESN'T FIT

On June 13, 1994, 12 hours
after a double homicide in
Brentwood, California, one
victim's ex was held for
questioning. The televised
trial of former grid star O.J.
Simpson, 47, the next year
became a three-ring judicial
circus in which lawyers,
witnesses, even the judge
did pratfalls. The evidence
trickling out over 36 weeks
convinced jurors that yes,
they must acquit.

JOHN BARR / LIAISON

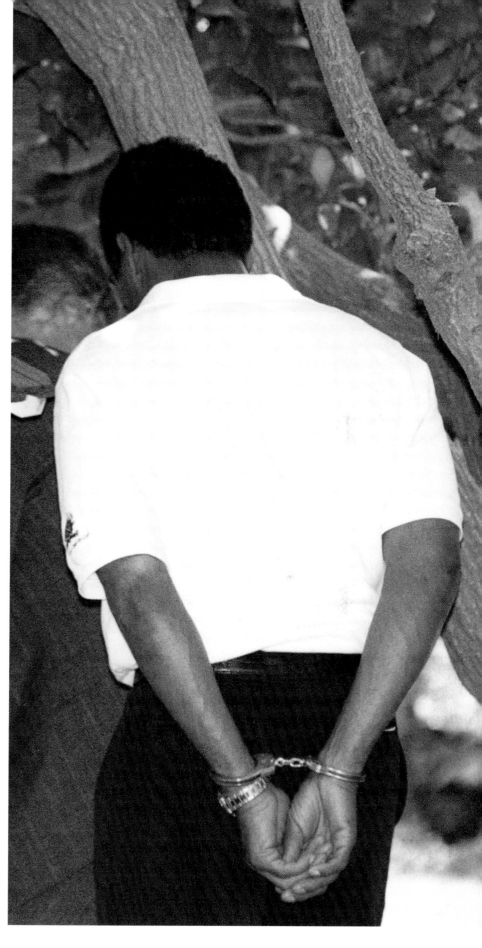

CLOUDS OF DOOM

Tannie Shannon, cradling granddaughter Andrea, and wife Frances, leading the family pet, sought high ground after the floodgates to Texas's Lake Conroe had to be opened in October 1994 after three days of torrential rain. By then, the Lower 48 was heeding the Weather Channel. In 1989, Hurricane Hugo blitzed the Carolinas. Hurricane Andrew, which sliced across South Florida and Louisiana in 1992, was worse. And in 1993, the Mississippi River, swollen by 100 days of rain, flooded parts of nine states and left 70,000 homeless.

DAVID LEESON /
DALLAS MORNING NEWS

THE ENEMY WAS US

A federal office building in Oklahoma City was felled on April 19, 1995 (above), by a truck bomb that killed 168 — among them, 19 tots in a child-care center — and injured 850. Home-brewing the explosive from feed-store chemicals and highly combustible racing fuel: homegrown terrorist Timothy McVeigh, 28 (right, with his lawyer during a 1996 pretrial interview). The Desert Storm veteran believed in the far-right radicalism of a crazy quilt of militiamen, survivalists and others. Oklahoma City was his answer to Waco, Texas, where, beset by federal agents, 75 members of survivalist David Koresh's cult had died on April 19, 1993. For his crime, McVeigh received the death penalty.

ABOVE: JIM ARGO / DAILY
OKLAHOMAN / SABA
RIGHT: ROBBIE McCLARAN

Our Family Tree

The past roars with things to tell us. We have begun to hear, thanks to 20th Century know-how. These days, a chip of bone, a fretted flint, a petrified seed can be scanned like bar codes for date of origin. So we are able to push back ever further in our century-long search for the missing link, that mutational species of primates evolving into Homo sapiens. We've also refound some long-lost kin. Guess what? Even the earliest bonded. And cocooned. And lit fires. And buried their dead. And made war — and art (below). Which is to say, they stopped dragging their knuckles much earlier than we so smugly thought. How's this for a notion: We'd be hardly more awkward around a native of way-back-when than we are visiting a country where the natives speak a different tongue.

THE FIRST PICTURE SHOW

Late in 1994, three French spelunkers became the first visitors to an underground gallery in 30,000 years. The cave paintings at Vallon-Pont-d'Arc in south-eastern France are more sophisticated than those of the Lascaux Grotto (done 17,000 years later). Of the images, 415 are of animals — and one of a bison whose legs are clearly human.

JEAN CLOTTES / SYGMA

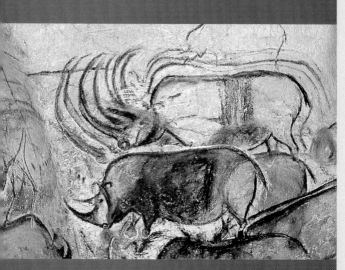

A MONKEY'S AUNT

Fossil fragments found on Piltdown Common, Sussex, rocked the world when, in 1912, the reconstructed skull at right was pronounced that of "the missing link"! Who had lived in England! Alas, tests in the 1950s showed the cranium to be a woman's and the jawbone an orangutan's. Piltdown Man was a hoax. Whodunit? One suspect: mysterian Arthur Conan Doyle (see page 157).

ARCHIVE PHOTOS

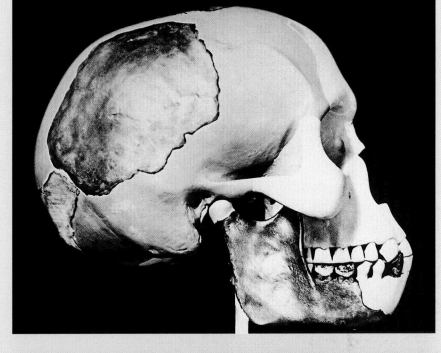

REAL-LIFE FLINTSTONE

From 1927 on, paleontologists began to find, in caves near Peking, a trove of skeletal remains more than 400,000 years old. They also unearthed tools and singed animal bones. Strikingly identical to modern humans from neck down, Peking Man had not much of a forehead. (Its brain averaged four-fifths the size of ours.) The original specimens vanished during the 1941 Japanese invasion of China; more have since been discovered.

AMERICAN MUSEUM OF NATURAL HISTORY

IN THE YEAR 2525 (B.C.)

The six-acre palace complex at Knossos on Crete (above) was the lifework of British archaeologist Arthur Evans (inset). Drawn to the island partly by the Greek myth of the Minotaur, a half-bull, half-man monster, in 1900 he began to dig up a lost culture of maritime traders. The Minoans also worshiped bulls; and one of their written languages was a forerunner of Greek.

ABOVE: GORDON GAHAN / NGS IMAGE COLLECTION
LEFT: TIME INC.

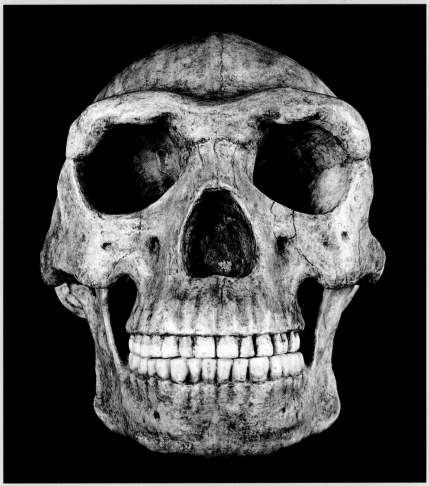

A CITY IN THE CLOUDS

Yale historian Hiram Bingham (an Indiana Jones prototype) was searching the Peruvian highlands for a legendary lost Inca city in 1911 when he came upon Machu Picchu (above). It was a key ceremonial center for the advanced civilization that ruled much of the Andes for 200-plus years before its 16th Century conquest, in just 40 years, by Spain.

TIME INC.

BEST FACE FORWARD

Thirty-three centuries after his reign in Egypt ended, Tutankhamen's burial place was unsealed (see page 93). In 1976, the Boy King's gilded sarcophagus mask was the gaudiest of 55 relics sent on a six-city U.S. tour. Museums were SRO with crowds gawking at the gold sculptures, alabaster vases and jewelry. And to think — Tut was a lesser pharaoh.

WALTER SANDERS / LIFE

DINNER AT EIGHT

Beginning with his dig at the Iraqi site of Ur in 1922, Leonard Woolley (above right) reversed the cruel loot-and-run philosophy of fieldwork. The British archaeologist documented each find, no matter how small. Among his prizes from Ur: the above inlaid panel showing a royal banquet circa 2500 B.C., when the pre-Babylonian kingdom of Sumer ruled ancient Mesopotamia.

ABOVE:
FRANK SCHERSCHEL / LIFE
ABOVE RIGHT:
CORBIS / BETTMANN-UPI

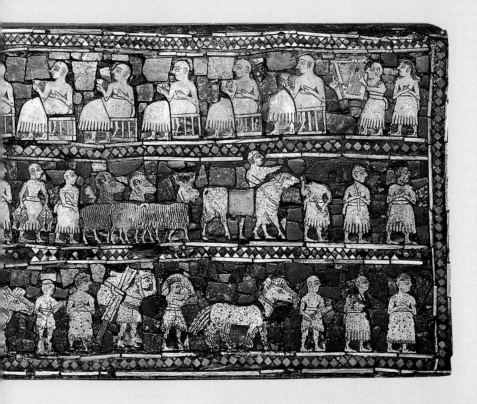

CURIOUS GEORGE NO. 1

The year Lindy soloed the Pond, another aviator noticed animals like a 100-yard-long monkey (right) etched into a high desert in southern Peru, as well as far larger geometric shapes. There are some 800 miles of Nazca Lines, drawn probably about the time of Christ by persons unknown. How had earthbound artists gained the perspective to plan some 300 meticulous geoglyphs? They didn't, said Erich von Daniken in his 1969 best-seller, *Chariot of the Gods?*; it was done by visiting aliens. Mix in a little Roswell fever and presto: *The X-Files*.

WILLIAM ALBERT ALLARD /
NGS IMAGE COLLECTION

PRESENT AT THE CREATION

Two millennia ago, near Khirbat Qumran by the Dead Sea, a clay urn (left, after restoration) containing some leather scrolls was placed in a cave. It was found in 1947 by young Bedouins. Though the leather had split (below left), the Hebraic script was legible. The scrolls (plus others found nearby) were worth unfragmenting: The texts give a firsthand look, from the epicenter, of the emergence of Christianity from its Judaic roots.

LEFT: CORBIS / BETTMANN- UPI
BELOW LEFT:
LARRY BURROWS / LIFE

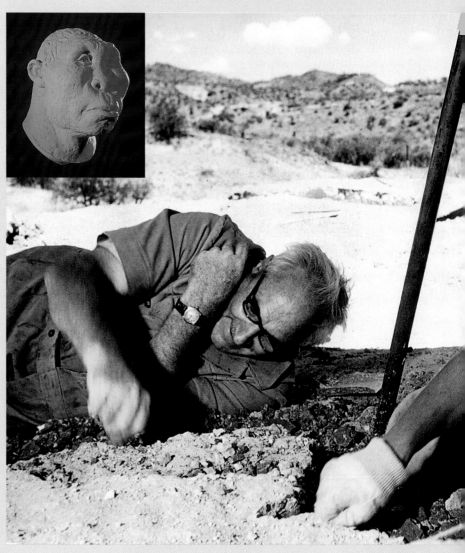

A SPLASHY VOYAGE

Norwegian ethnologist Thor Heyerdahl, 32, made news in 1947 when he and a five-man crew sailed a balsa-log raft, *Kon-Tiki*, from Peru to a Polynesian isle in 101 days. Why? To show that perhaps it had been South Americans, not Asians, who first peopled the mid-Pacific archipelagos. As science, it was dubious; as a recruiting poster for anthropology, it was brilliant.

CORBIS / BETTMANN-INP

ETERNAL COMPANIONS

In 1974 farmers digging for water near Xi'an in northwest China struck historical gold: an imperial tomb filled with 6,000 bronze horses (right) and life-size terra cotta warriors (each with a unique face), and more. Shih Huang-ti rated the send-off; he had ordered work begun on a Wall that would eventually stretch 1,500 miles across China.

EASTFOTO /
XINHUA NEWS AGENCY

SURROGATE PARENTS

The hands-and-knees patience of British fossil hunters Louis and Mary Leakey yielded, in 1959, skull chips that forced a quantum revision of evolutionary theory. The fragments were of a tool-using hominid (re-creation, inset) who lived 1.75 million years ago in Tanzania's Olduvai Gorge; later finds pushed our earliest two-legged ancestors back to 4.4 million B.C.

ROBERT SISSON, ROBERT OAKES
(INSET) / NGS IMAGE COLLECTION

FROZEN IN TIME

One day 5,300 years ago a man of about 30, at right, was crossing the Tyrolean Alps when overtaken by a blizzard. His icy tomb did not thaw until 1991. So well preserved was he that we know his eye color (blue) and basic diet (milled grains). We also learned that in the Stone Age, some guys cut their hair short and sported tattoos.

GERHARD HINTERLEITNER /
LIAISON

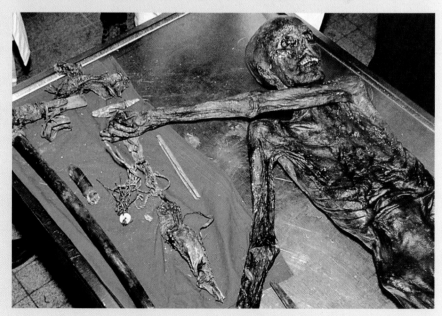

THE TELLTALE JIGSAW

Only by meticulously reconstructing debris from a fallen 747 were federal investigators able to analyze a disaster that spooked America. In July 1996, with terrorists threatening to disrupt the Atlanta Olympics, TWA Flight 800 had just left New York for Paris when it blew up in midair. By December 1997, the chief suspect was a subtle design flaw.

JEFF CHRISTENSEN / REUTERS / ARCHIVE PHOTOS

AN EARLY ENCOUNTER

On the White House rope line in summer 1995 was West Wing intern Monica Lewinsky, 22. What transpired between her and Bill Clinton is graphically documented in independent counsel Kenneth Starr's 1998 report, whose juicy parts made it sell like hotcakes. In 1999, after the President survived impeachment, a quicky bio of Monica hit bookstores. It sold like lukewarmcakes.

SYGMA

STAND AND DELIVER

If those from Venus could have a new artifice (the Wonderbra), so could those from Mars (Viagra, to ensure that old soldiers don't fade away). This was one blue bomber even antidruggies like Bob Dole could endorse. By 1999, seven states had said that any medical insurer covering a cure for male erectile dysfunction must also reimburse the costs of female contraception.

ED GABLE / TIME

BURNING BRIGHT

On April 13, 1997, Tiger Woods, 21 (below, accepting his Masters jacket from outgoing champ Nick Faldo), became the first African-Asian-American to take one of golf's major titles. The Augusta course where he won was, until 1975, closed to people of color unless they were caddies. On tour, Woods would still occasionally hear racist barbs not aimed at the Thai portion of his heritage.

JOHN BIEVER / SPORTS ILLUSTRATED

> LET'S GO TO THE VIDEOTAPE

Michael Jordan, unlike Alexander the Great, retired when he had no worlds left to conquer. Six titles in 13 years — including a second threepeat in June 1998 — and 29,277 points. So in early 1999 (with wife Juanita's O.K., as long as no more baseball), he rejected $21.2 million and went about his businesses. If Michael, 35, looked choked up, consider the NBA: It had no Air apparent.

JOHN BIEVER /
SPORTS ILLUSTRATED

< THE STARR CHAMBER

The president is a perjurer, and that's illegal, Kenneth Starr, 52, warned a House panel in November 1998. Starr had been appointed, under a Watergate-era act, to hunt for executive misconduct; his probe into a land scam resulted, four years later, in charges of sex and lies on videotape. The House impeached. The Senate acquitted. Starr was the last of two dozen independent counsels; Congress let the act lapse in 1999.

DAVID BURNETT / CONTACT

> A NEW CHASE BEGINS

Thirty-seven seasons after their dad hit a benchmark 61 home runs, Kevin Maris, 38 (near right), and brother Roger Jr., 39, greeted Mark McGwire, who had just nailed number 62. It was a year for going yard. Chicago Cub Sammy Sosa finished 1998 with 66, but McGwire, 34, outbashed him by four.

JOHN BIEVER /
SPORTS ILLUSTRATED

CUBA LIBRE? NOT TODAY

Fidel Castro, 71, soft-ened his antireligion policies six years earlier, but he was in no mood for the sermon delivered by John Paul II, 77, on a papal visit to Cuba in January 1998. The pontiff criticized his host's poor human rights record. However, he also criticized the U.S. economic sanctions against Cuba, levied in 1962, "because they hurt the most needy."

ANTONIO RIBEIRO / LIAISON

HOMOPHOBIA ON THE RANGE

Lured from a straight bar in Laramie, Wyoming, a gay college student was roped to this fence in October 1998 after being beaten, burned and robbed. Matthew Shepard, 21, was barely alive when found after 18 hours. His death five days later was cheered on a Web site run by a Kansas minister: godhatesfags.com.

STEVE LISS / TIME

UNCONTROLLED GUNS

On a hilltop in Littleton, Colorado, stood crosses for the 15 victims of an April 1999 high school massacre. Included were two for the young shooters (one at far right), who also wounded 23 (among them, Patrick Ireland, inset). The pro-gun NRA lamented this, as well as seven earlier student rampages that killed 17, but then opened its convention in nearby Denver anyway.

KEVIN MOLONEY / LIAISON
INSET: CNN

>
THE WHITE PEARL

As Pelé, Brazil's Black Pearl, ruled men's soccer a third of a century ago, so America's Mia Hamm, 27, has dominated the rising women's game. The Air Force brat was also the most visible beneficiary of Title IX, a law enacted three months after her birth that required colleges to fund women's sports. Hamm led Team USA to the 1999 Women's World Cup finals. They won.

CHUCK SOLOMON /
SPORTS ILLUSTRATED

<
NO PLACE LIKE HOME

Welcoming a U.N. peace-keeper to Kosovo province in Yugoslavia in June 1999 was no stretch for these kids; restoring their lives would be. They and fellow ethnic Albanians had been targeted for "cleansing" by Belgrade. It was the latest sad chapter of a seven-year, religion-fueled civil war ruining the nation that had hosted 1984's sparkling Winter Games at Sarajevo.

YANNIS BEHRAKIS / REUTERS /
ARCHIVE PHOTOS

>
WHAT'S THE NEXT MOVE?

By June 1999, Hillary Rodham Clinton, 51, and her husband, Bill, 52, had lived in public housing for 16 straight years. (Daughter Chelsea grew up without a place to call home.) Now their latest lease was nearing its end. Buy or rent? Because even if certain events were to keep them inside the Beltway, members of the Senate are not entitled to free digs.

STEPHEN JAFFE /
CORBIS / BETTMANN-AFP

A GRRRL NAMED SUE

Air Jordan was grounded so the Second City turned its lonely eyes to another bigfoot (right, as modeled by paleontologists). Some 67 million years ago, the 40-foot-long, five-ton Sue — after Susan Hendrickson, who discovered the amazing fossil in 1990; its gender is unknown — ruled what is now South Dakota. Its 300-plus bones having been reattached, the T-rex is now ready to rule Chicago's Field Museum.

IRA BLOCK /
NGS IMAGE COLLECTION

REQUIEM

JACQUELINE KENNEDY ONASSIS, 1929–1994

The woman even world leaders called Jackie (to her discomfort) never shed a public tear despite reversals to make Sophocles weep. Two high-profile yet vacant marriages were by her design; one stillborn child, a second who lived but 40 hours and presidential widowhood were not. She was a working girl early and late in life. Her professional legacy does not draw our eye. Her personal grace surely does.

BILL EPPRIDGE / LIFE

JERRY GARCIA 1942–1995

In Jerry's 30 years fronting the band, the Grateful Dead lived on tour, giving free-form concerts — powered by his extended guitar jams — that left fans glassy-eyed. Even those who were clean. Cherry Garcia was a witty name for an ice cream flavor, though he probably preferred Heavenly Hash. Garcia never did kick his drug habit; he was in rehab when the heart attack hit.

HENRY GROSSMAN

AUDREY HEPBURN 1929–1993

Her elfin charm, Euro-tinged English and swan's neck were captivating in movies from *Roman Holiday* to *My Fair Lady* to *Breakfast at Tiffany's*. When her career waned, Hepburn (who once subsisted on ground-up tulip bulbs in Nazi-ruled Holland) took on the role of UNICEF ambassador. While visiting famine victims in Somalia, she began to feel weak. It was cancer.

BOB WILLOUGHBY

CESAR CHAVEZ
1927–1993

He taught Anglo-Americans the word *huelga*, or strike. Born in Yuma, Arizona, to migrant workers, he himself was a stoop laborer except for a Navy stint during World War II. In 1965, Chavez began a strike against California grape growers that was won in 1970. He soon organized other agribiz workers and, in 1977, even took on the Teamsters — and beat them.

BILL EPPRIDGE / LIFE

WILMA RUDOLPH
1940–1994

First she outran polio. Then she outran an impoverished childhood in rural Tennessee. In 1960, at the Rome Olympics, she outran the competition in the 100- and 200-meters, as well as in the sprint relay, to become the first American woman to win three golds at one Games. After hanging up her spikes, Rudolph worked in inner cities, showing kids the fastest way out.

MARK KAUFFMAN / LIFE

GEORGE BURNS
1896–1996

During his first career, which arced from vaudeville to radio to early TV, he was straight man for wife and comedy partner Gracie Allen (left). After her 1958 retirement, Burns claimed the punch lines — and delivered them winningly in movies (*The Sunshine Boys, Oh God*) and late-night talk shows until it was time to say, Good night, George. Good night, George.

ARCHIVE PHOTOS

JOHN F. KENNEDY JR.
1960–1999

Born two months before his family moved into the White House, the child spent his third birthday helping bury a dad hardly known. Kennedy did not enter politics despite his bloodlines and a surfeit of personal glamour, preferring to co-found a public affairs magazine. En route to a cousin's wedding the plane he was piloting crashed; on board were wife Carolyn, 33 (right), and sister-in-law Lauren Bessette.

DENIS REGGIE

ARTHUR ASHE
1943–1993

In 1968, he became the last amateur and first black to win the U.S. Open men's singles. When heart disease cut short his tennis career, Ashe took up an activism fostered by having to learn the game on segregated courts in Richmond, Virginia. To civil rights he would add championing other victims of AIDS, which he had contracted through a tainted transfusion.

JOHN ZIMMERMAN / LIFE

ALFRED EISENSTAEDT
1898–1995

On Martha's Vineyard in 1954 Eisie gazed into the other side of the lens. A German Jew, he arrived in the U.S. in time to become a charter *Life* photojournalist. His signature image was the Smooch (see page 214), but he also covered war, Americana, Hollywood and world leaders. The title of a 1966 anthology summed him up best: *Witness to Our Time*.

ALFRED EISENSTAEDT / LIFE

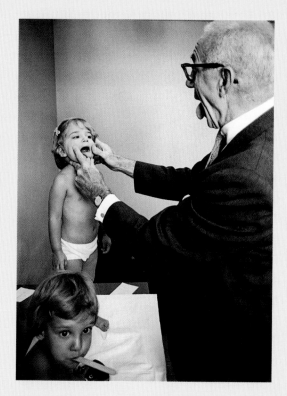

BENJAMIN SPOCK
1903–1998

The Common Sense Book of Baby and Child Care came out in 1946 — just in time for parents busy launching the Baby Boom. Thus was the consulting pediatrician to a generation blamed when some feed-on-demanders grew into hippies (or worse). Dr. Spock decided a second opinion was needed, so he shut his practice and joined the anti-Vietnam movement.

BOB GOMEL / LIFE

MOTHER TERESA
1910–1997

Along with a healer's hand, she had a fund-raiser's gift for publicizing her empire of charity (right, with Princess Diana in 1997). At 18, Agnes Gonxha Bojaxhiu was sent by a Catholic order to India. Twenty years later, she and her nuns began to tend the leprous, the maimed, the dying. By the time Mother Teresa won a 1979 Nobel, she oversaw 250 centers worldwide.

DIANA, PRINCESS OF WALES
1961–1997

At age 19, she accepted the proposal of a prince of the realm. What followed was as if from a rock classic: *Every move you make / Every vow you break / Every smile you fake / Every claim you stake. . . .* Yes, we were watching her, always. And we saw an adult life that began as a sanitized fairy tale conclude with a death macabre enough for the Brothers Grimm.

MIKE SEGAR / REUTERS / ARCHIVE PHOTOS

Extended Picture Credits

While every effort has been made to give appropriate credit for photographs and illustrations reproduced in this book, the publishers will be pleased to rectify any omissions or inaccuracies in the next printing.

Page ii: NASA

Page 8, bottom: AMNH negative #336289, photocopy – P. Goldberg, courtesy Department of Library Services, American Museum of Natural History.

Page 16: Steinbrugge Collection, Earthquake Engineering Research Center, University of California, Berkeley.

Page 17, top: Picasso, Pablo; "Les Demoiselles d'Avignon." Paris (June–July 1907). Oil on canvas, 8' by 7'8" (243.9 by 233.7 cm). The Museum of Modern Art, New York. Acquired through the Lillie P. Bliss Bequest. Photograph, 1999, The Museum of Modern Art, New York.

Page 19: Millstein Division of U.S. History, Local History & Genealogy, The New York Public Library, Astor, Lenox and Tilden Foundations.

Page 20: Millstein Division of U.S. History, Local History & Genealogy, The New York Public Library, Astor, Lenox and Tilden Foundations.

Page 21, top: Brown Brothers.

Page 25, top: Millstein Division of U.S. History, Local History & Genealogy, The New York Public Library, Astor, Lenox and Tilden Foundations.

Page 29, top right: Courtesy of Colorado Historical Society, negative #F4715.

Page 37, top: Canadian National / Illinois Central.

Page 52, top right and bottom left: Harry Ransom Humanities Research Center, The University of Texas at Austin.

Page 55, top right: Halsman Estate.

Page 77, top right: S0117495, 40-12-05/10, color transparency. Bazille, Frédéric (1841–1870). Pierre Auguste Renoir, painter. Oil on canvas, 1867. 62 x 51 cm. Musée d'Orsay, Paris, France.

Page 81: Romana Javitz Collection, Miriam and Ira D. Wallach Division of Arts, Prints and Photographs, The New York Public Library, Astor, Lenox and Tilden Foundations.

Page 93, bottom: Photography by Egyptian Expedition, the Metropolitan Museum of Art.

Page 134: Vandamm Studio, The New York Public Library for the Performing Arts, The Billy Rose Theatre Collection.

Page 136, top: Dever / Black Star.

Page 146, bottom left: AMNH negative #325024, courtesy Department of Library Services, American Museum of Natural History.

Page 154, top left: Dever / Black Star.

Page 157, right: Liaison Agency.

Page 159, right: Reprinted with permission of Joanna T. Steichen.

Page 187: Mondrian, Piet; "Broadway Boogie Woogie" (1942–43). Oil on Canvas, 50 x 50" (127 x 127 cm). The Museum of Modern Art, New York. Given anonymously. Photograph © 1999 the Museum of Modern Art, New York.

Page 217, bottom: S0075506, 40-12-11/66, color transparency. Munch, Edvard (1863–1944). "Self-Portrait, the Night," 1923. Munch Museum, Oslo, Norway.

Page 219, top left: Photograph, DN-003882, Emma Goldman, Chicago (Ill.), 1906; Photographer – Chicago Daily News Collection.

Page 230: Harry Ransom Humanities Research Center, Photography Collection, The University of Texas at Austin.

Page 239, top right: Harry Ransom Humanities Research Center, Photography Collection, The University of Texas at Austin.

Page 276, top right: S0114138, OC54.002, color transparency. Warhol, Andy (1928–1987). "Campbell's Soup Can, 19¢," 1962. Synthetic polymer paint and silkscreen ink and graphite on canvas; 72 by 54 inches.

Page 403, bottom: AMNH negative #315447, courtesy Department of Library Services, American Museum of Natural History.

Page 424: Material created with support to AURA/ST ScI from NASA-26555 is reproduced here with permission. Courtesy of Jeff Hester and Paul Scowen (Arizona State University) and NASA.

LIFE: Our Century in Pictures

Editor: Richard B. Stolley
Deputy Editor and Writer: Tony Chiu
Designer: Susan Marsh
Picture Editor: Debra Cohen
Researcher: Carol Weil
Copy Editor: Richard McAdams
Associate Writer: Leslie Jay

Special thanks to Sheilah Scully, Ellen Graham, Gretchen Wessels (photo researchers), Kelli Green, Daniel Chui (scanners), Pamela Wilson, Annette Rusin, Brenda Cherry (researchers), Jill Jaroff (copy editor), Delia Chiu (indexer), Sally Proudfit, Bob Jackson, Helene Veret, and Jennifer McAlwee.

Produced in cooperation with Time Inc. Editorial Services

Director: Sheldon Czapnik
Research Center: Lany McDonald
Picture Collection:
Beth Iskander, Kathi Doak
Photo Lab: Tom Hubbard
Time-Life Syndication:
Maryann Kornely

Life Magazine

Managing Editor: Isolde Motley
Publisher: Donald B. Fries

Published by Time Warner Trade Publishing

Chairman, Time Warner Trade Publishing: Laurence J. Kirshbaum
Publisher, Bulfinch Press:
Carol Judy Leslie
Senior Editor, Bulfinch Press:
Terry Reece Hackford
Production Manager,
Bulfinch Press: Sandra Klimt

Bulfinch Press is an imprint and trademark of Little, Brown and Company (Inc.)

FIRST SPECIAL SALES EDITION:
August 2006
Second Printing, 2007
ISBN-978-0-08212-5865-1
PRINTED IN THE
UNITED STATES OF AMERICA

Seven thousand years ago, this is how one sector of the Milky Way looked.

Thanks to certain advances on earth in the last 100 years, we are able to capture light that

originated in deep space, and the deep past, and to interpret the snapshot (taken by the Hubble

telescope, orbiting above atmospheric distortion since 1990). Shown is a pillar of matter

in the Eagle Nebula. Within this celestial womb, stars are being born.

HESTER AND SCOWAN / NASA

LIFE: OUR CENTURY IN PICTURES

DESIGNED BY SUSAN MARSH

PICTURES EDITED BY DEBRA COHEN

COMPOSED IN META AND ITC BODONI BY RICHARD MCADAMS AND SUSAN MARSH

SEPARATIONS BY PROFESSIONAL GRAPHICS INC., ROCKFORD, ILLINOIS